From Scepticism to Hope

(One Black-led Church's Response to Social Responsibility)

by Selwyn Arnold

National Overseer of the New Testament Church of God

with a Commendation by the Archbishop of Canterbury
and a Foreword by Prebendary Pat Dearnley and Bishop Wilfred Wood

Dedication
To
MY PARENTS
who first taught me to pray and
instilled within me by precept and example
a love for God and his Word
and
to my only son, Selwyn Jnr., whom I love as God's special gift ·
and to
Muriel Joyce
my dear wife and faithful co-worker
this work is gratefully dedicated

THE COVER PICTURE
is a design by Tim Bryan

First Impression July 1992
ISBN 1 85174 213 1

GROVE BOOKS LIMITED
Bramcote   Nottingham   NG9 3DS

CONTENTS

Commendation

by Dr. George Carey, the Archbishop of Canterbury

One of the newer features of the British Churches' scene has been the emergence of the 'Black-led' Churches. This was not well charted, and certainly not well known at first-hand, by many in the historic denominations of this land until very recently; and it is likely that it is the inclusion of these Churches within the fellowship of Churches Together in England (CTE) and the Council of Churches of Britain and Ireland (CCBI), both of them inaugurated in September 1990, which has brought the 'black-led' churches into the limelight.

The book which follows charts an internal reorientation which has been going on within the New Testament Church of God over recent years, matching the advance in its external relationships and image. On a somewhat smaller scale this change reflects the concerns of the Church of England's *Faith in the City*, the report of my predecessor's Commission on Urban Priority Areas. It is indeed (to our shame as a nation) largely within Urban Priority Areas that 'black-led' churches are to be found—springing as they do from deprived ethnic communities. It is in those areas that the New Testament Church of God has had to work out the this-worldly implications of what had been previously held to be a largely other-worldly gospel of Jesus Christ. It is a moving story.

From the point of view of the Church of England, I cannot but note how far distant and irrelevant we have seemed to be from the New Testament Church of God anbd its recent history recorded here. That being so, I am the more delighted that Bishop Selwyn Arnold, when he was seeking a publisher, should have approached an Anglican bishop, Colin Buchanan, whose role as honorary manager of Grove Books Limited is well-known. It appears that he had been a friend of the New Testament Church of God in Handsworth in Birmingham ever since the riots and fires recorded here on page 71 below, and this led to their confidence being placed in him. It is correspondingly appropriate that a Foreword should be contributed jointly by Bishop Wilfred Wood, the first black bishop of the Church of England, and first chairman of the Committee for Black Anglican Concerns, and by Prebendary Pat Dearnley who did a tremendous job for the Church of England through four years as the Archbishop's Officer for Urban Priority Areas. I greatly hope that the participation of these notable leaders from the Church of England betokens both a greater understanding on our part of the 'black-led' Churches, and a loving desire to break down all racist barriers which might still hold black and white apart even whilst they name the name of the same Lord Jesus Christ. May this book open many eyes.

George Carey, Archbishop of Canterbury
July 1992

Foreword

by Prebendary Pat Dearnley and Bishop Wilfred Wood

We are delighted to join together in acclaiming Bishop Selwyn Arnold's book, which we believe may prove to be a milestone in the story of British Christianity. Our own perspective is that of the Archbishop's Officer for Urban Priority Areas and of a Black Anglican 'immigrant' who came from Barbados in 1962, and has been since 1985 a bishop in the Church of England.

Surveying the religious background to English urban priority areas for the report *Faith In The City* (first published December 1985) the Archbishop's Commission noted 'The rise of the black-led churches has been dramatic.' (*FITC* 2.54). In stark contrast to the declining membership of the mainstream denominations the Commission recorded an average annual growth rate for the black churches of 5 per cent. The membership of the New Testament Church of God doubled between 1966 and 1970 and has maintained a healthy growth rate ever since. This very book, *From Scepticism to Hope*, bears witness to this. While Bishop Arnold's study focusses on this Church, the general features he describes are characteristic of the majority of denominations (approaching 200 in total) which comprises the sector designated 'black' or 'black-led' churches. (This title has, of course, arisen within predominantly 'white' British society.)

Bishop Arnold is careful to note in his opening chapter that most of the original black churches were already established in other parts of the world and some of their adherents were among the first generation of immigrants to Britain. But unquestionably it was the lack of genuine Christian love and fellowship on the part of the host community which was the decisive factor in promoting the burgeoning growth of black congregations. This sad fact was recognized and emphasized repeatedly at meetings held in dioceses, deaneries and parishes to follow up the ACUPA Report. Rarely did anyone have the courage to ask the present company how *they* might have reacted when faced with a sudden influx of black faces into their own congregations. One fears that some of the latent reserve and even hostility shown by previous generations of British worshippers in the 1950s is by no means dead and buried in the 1990s.

However, it is also important to avoid the false assumption that all Afro-Caribbean Christians are in some sense 'lapsed' Anglicans, RCs, Methodists etc. At one meeting to discuss *FITC* issues one of us heard a black priest arguing along these lines, and referring derisively to members of black-led churches as 'clap hands Christians'. Mercifully such an unhelpful stereotype is not shared by the majority of black members within the mainstream denominations. Their spokespersons have understandably been particularly concerned with efforts to increase black representation in synods and decision-making bodies of their own churches. At the same time they have not hesitated to urge their church bodies to be more generous in sharing resources with black-led congregations, notably in the matter of making premises available for worship and other gatherings. Thus the report *Seeds of Hope* (GS972 published in 1991 by the General Synod) includes specific recommendations (5.43, 44) to the Anglican dioceses on this issue.

Hopefully those responsible for promoting black concerns within their own churches will encourage the circulation of Bishop Arnold's survey. It will prove a significant contribution to the efforts being made at local levels towards closer relationships between mainstream and black-led churches. One of my greatest disappointments in the initial stages of follow-up to the ACUPA report was our failure to involve the black-led churches in the process. No doubt this reflected the existing situation in local areas. At least there is some encouragement to be drawn from the growing recognition among church leaders that it simply will not forward desired goals of unity for solidly white committee to arrange programmes and then bemoan the fact that black neighbours did not respond to invitations to join. For real partnership develop there must be full participation in planning processes from the outset.

Selwyn Arnold's study appears at a crucial time in the history of the Afro-Caribbean population of the United Kingdom. In an address to the 1991 Annual Conference of Evangelical Christians for Racial Justice Pastor Joel Edwards outlined four stages in the growth of the urban black churches in Britain. The first stage, 'Inception', coincided with the arrival of the first immigrants who struggled to survive in an alien situation. Stage two, 'Consolidation', saw the establishment of black-led church headquarters and an increasing concern to develop infrastructures within the churches. The third stage, 'Initiation', which Pastor Edwards locates in the late 70s and during the 80s, witnessed a process of escalating community involvement and social action. It is particularly this period that Selwyn Arnold charts in his present study.

We have now entered a fourth stage termed 'Dynamic Transition', in which, according to Joel Edwards, 'We are beginning to look at the label "Black Church" much more seriously. We are now asking ourselves what the label means; are the implications and ramifications of being called a Black Church?'. This emerging critical self-awareness was evident among those gathered for a Black Pastors Conference Pat Dearnley was invited to address on *Faith In The City*. In discussion the familiar problems were aired—the need to raise funds to maintain the churches; the niggardly attitudes of white church officers over the hire of their church halls; and the increasing cri-de-coeur by many regarding the defection of young black people from attendance at church and their rejection of the 'traditions of the elders'. But alongside these issues a new agenda was being raised. The significant ones articulated at that conference were also raised on other occasions under the *Faith In The City* umbrella when the subject of black-led-churches was discussed. Ironically this sometimes happened when the participants were themselves all white with no black representatives of mainstream, let alone black-led, churches present! We refer briefly to five of these which we suggest Selwyn Arnold and all who share his concerns need to address.

(i) THE THEOLOGICAL STANCE OF THE BLACK-LED CHURCHES VIS-A-VIS THE MAINSTREAM DENOMINATIONS

As Selwyn Arnold indicates, the theology of the New Testament Church of God and most black-led churches is very conservative, often more so than that of evangelicals who belong to the mainstream churches and share similar convictions about the authority of Scripture. It is ecumenical bad manners for members of the recognized denominations publicly to criticize the theology of the black churches. We have heard clergy who hold liberal or radical views of the Bible privately dismissing the thology of their black neighbours as 'fundamentalist' or 'naive' e.g. in relation to eschatology, spirituality ('holiness'), worship etc. The implications of this for co-operation in local councils of churches, ministers' fraternals and similar bodies are considerable.

(ii) THE MISSIOLOGICAL QUESTIONS POSED BY THE CONGREGAIONAL STRUCTURES OF BLACK-LED CHURCHES

The authors of *Faith In The City* were emphatic that they wished to see churches in UPAs which were 'local, participating and outward-looking'. These 'notes' are regrettably not always true of many black-led churches, which operate on the gathered church principle and sometimes have little roots in the communities where they gather for Sunday worship and other meetings. Often worshippers are collected by minibus from a wide geographical area. One incumbent of a parish whose premises were hired each Sunday by a black church told one of us that if the minibus broke down there was no service, for none of the congregaion lived within walking distance of the hall. In the long-term, how satisfactory can this practice be for establsihing strong, locally-rooted churches which are able to nourish their members in mission among their neighbours? Yet these churches are never, as far as we know, exclusive, and the 'brave' white person who chooses to join is enthusiastically welcomed. This is in direct contrast to the experiences of the other of us who, when a vicar, had doors slammed in his face because of his colour.

(iii) THE ABSENCE OF MEMBERS OF THE BLACK-LED CHURCHES FROM THE CHAMBERS OF NATIONAL AND LOCAL GOVERNMENT

Some little impetus has been given to the cause of racial integration in the U.K. by the election of articulate black representatives to the Westminster Parliament and various local councils. However in most cases where such representatives profess a Christian allegiance it is to one of the mainstream denominations. Doubtless the legacy of the 'holiness movement', with its suspicion of politics as heavily tainted by 'the world', is largely to blame for the reluctance of Christians from black-led Churches to enter the arena of secular politics. It is certainly *not* due to any lack of the capability which many possess to be articulate and inspiring leaders within their communities. All of us who are anxious that Christian perspectives should be brought to bear on political, social and economic issues must encourage our friends in the black-led churches to address this matter. The theological thrust of this book would point in that direction, and we long that such people should emerge.

(iv) THE INEVITABLE EMERGES OF A BLACK MIDDLE CLASS

For almost four decades the basic membership of black-led churches has been drawn from those in the lower income groups of our society. The children and grandchildren of the first generation of immigrants are no longer content to take jobs as transport workers, hospital ancillary staff, etc. Despite the indices of educational deprivation, they aspire to, and will assuredly attain, positions as lawyers, teachers, accountants and so on. Whether or not John Major's vision of a 'classless society' proves a reality, the close of the current decade will see the establishment of a sizeable proportion of black people within the professions. Where will the committed Christians among them find their spiritual home? We cannot forbear reflecting on the pilgrimage of many Christians from working-class backgrounds in the Salvation Army, Pentecostal and other chapels to respectable Anglicanism or Free Churches! Will history repeat itself among the coming generation of black Christians?

(v) THE ULTIMATE CHALLENGE OF MULTI-ETHNIC AND MULTI-CULTURAL CHURCHES

The previous point leads directly to this last one. It was raised at a *Faith in the City* meeting one of us attended in a southern suburban deanery where all the faces present were white. When mention of black-led churches came up one man rose and quoting St. Paul in Galatians 2.28 asked simply: 'Do you think that the existence of separate black congregations is God's will for the Church?' Adroitly the speaker turned this back into a question for the ensuing group discussion! It is a crucial question, for it goes to the heart of the gospel's claim to unite people across the frontiers of race, class and culture. From the standpoint of the black-led churches we know of no case where white members are not welcomed to the fellowship, and we have known several white Christians who worship with black congregations on a weekly basis. If as Christians we are to contribute to and be heard by our multi-ethnic society (not just in UPAs) we shall have to re-examine the rationale for continuing homogeneous congregations, whether black or white.

Whilst at theological college (Pat Dearnley) once heard a fellow student, Janani Luwum (later to be martyred as Archbishop of Uganda) say: 'You can play some sort of tune on only the white notes of a keyboard, and some sort of a tune on the black notes. But to get true harmony you have to play the black and white notes together.' Nearly thirty years later, reflecting on the contemporary church scene in Britain, we are both still haunted by those words. But such a harmony requires a mutual confidence which has hardly begun in England to-day. We long that this valuable study should help contribute to it. In particular we ask Christians of the older denominations to read, mark, learn and inwardly digest it.

Patrick Dearnley
Wilfred Wood

Preface

FROM SCEPTICISM TO HOPE is a reality to be prudently addressed by the New Testament Church of God (NTCG), and the wider Black-led Churches in the United Kingdom. The Church's hope lies in the belief in the imminent return of Jesus Christ to reign on earth for a thousand years, after which there will be a final judgement and the restoration of all things. This belief has had an unintended negative effect on the Church in that its aims and objectives have been to prepare its people for that day of the Lord, and seemingly, it has neglected to prepare them to live and participate in the affairs of this society. Believing that apostasy and degeneration of this evil world is inevitable, they live and hope for the new world where righteousness shall reign, and racial injustice, prejudice and discrimination will end.

This has resulted in an ambivalence developing within the Church among those young and adult members who recognize the need for progress and self-achievement in the struggle for survival. On the one hand, there is the desire to be faithful to the NTCG and its theology, doctrinal principles and traditions. But, in some ways, these seem to conflict with changing values in this modern and technological society. This has led some to be sceptical of the direction the Church has taken over the years and the resulting effect on their future.

This response seeks to provide guidelines to the Church by examination of its mission and ministry in light of the social imperatives enshrined in the gospel of Christ and his kingdom as well as to suggest areas in which one could legitimately be involved without compromising one's faith.

While affirming its belief in an eschatological day of the Lord to come as a thief in the night, members need to be equipped to influence the social development of their own society in the here and now.

The term 'Black-led' may need some clarification, for the NTCG is not to be classified as a 'Black Church' within the context of the Black Church movement in North America. The term was a nomenclature ascribed to Churches with Black leadership and a majority Black membership by the indigenous Churches when they accepted the fact that the Churches were not cultic ghettoes for the practice of a supposed 'Black religion', but were legitimate branches of evangelical protestant orthodoxy led by Black clergy. Several years elapsed before the acceptance of this fact. However, for some indigenous White people, there are other elements that make up a Black-led Church, such as, spontaneous loud congregational praying, vibrant, if not emotional, singing and hand-clapping, and in some cases, ecstatic worship and speaking in unknown tongues.

Some have even believed that this type of worship is peculiar to Black people, and the average White British person regards the Church to be Black people's Church.

On the contrary, the NTCG embraces all races and cultures that accept its evangelical, Pentecostal teachings and meet the requirements for membership.

There is also a feeling among some of the younger membership who, in recent times, have been exposed to the Black Church and its struggle in America and

'Black Theology' in particular, that there should be more emphasis on Black Church concepts. As they observe growing racism and tensions within the British society, and even in the Church, some question whether the NTCG's hope, rooted in White theology, will provide the solutions to these current problems. Some harp on the fact that White theology sought to project inferiority on the Black race by insisting that Blacks were the descendants of Ham who was cursed by his father, Noah, and sentenced to permanent servitude (Genesis 9.20-28). They demand answers to their questions regarding the NTCG's stance on such issues, and seek assurance they will not be shelved by the Church's failure to address them. The time has come when the younger membership of the Church will not just accept answers purely inspired from a supposed anointing of the Spirit. They demand to see the issues clearly supported by proper hermeneutical handling of the Word of God.

It is anticipated that this response will clarify the NTCG's hope in an eschatological coming of the Lord for people of every nation, an acknowledgement of social responsibility in keeping with the imperatives in the gospel of Jesus Christ, and will remind its members that implicit among the criteria for receiving the Master's benediction and welcome into his kingdom will be:

'Come, you blessed of My Father (that is, you favoured of God and appointed to eternal salvation), inherit—receive as your own—the kingdom prepared for you from the foundation of the world. For I was hungry and you gave me food; I was thirsty and you gave Me something to drink; I was a stranger and you brought me together with yourselves and welcomed and entertained and lodged me; I was naked and you clothed me; I was sick and you visited me with help and ministering care; I was in prison and you visited me.

'. . . Truly, I tell you, in as far as you did it to one of the least (in the estimation of men) of these my brethren, you did it to me.' (Matthew 25. 34-36, 40. *The Amplified New Testament*).

1. Introduction

The association of Black people with Great Britain has often been regarded as a phenomenon of the Fifties. It was therefore with much interest that I read the following cutting from *the Observer* (a British daily) dated 4 October 1981, indicating that Black presence in Britain was much earlier than the Fifties. The clip stated:

'Black people first settled in England 1800 years ago, an international conference on the history of Blacks in Britain was told last week, writes Martin Bailey.

'They were African troops who had served with the Roman invaders and subsequently settled near York.

'Mr. Paul Edwards of Edinburgh University, says that some African soldiers remained here after they had been discharged from the Roman Army, "probably because they wanted to live with English women."

'He cited evidence from an important third century archaeological find at Trentholme, near York, where more than 30 skeletons, which bone specialists believe to be those of Negroes, have been discovered.

'A second century inscription found at Burgh on Sands near Carlisle also helps confirm the African presence in Britain. The inscription refers to a special contingent of several hundred North African troops who were stationed at Hadrian's wall.'[1]

Some historians argue that Black people have been a part of the British society for well over 400 years but their historicity has been purposely or mistakenly ignored over the centuries. The search for Black identity in more recent times has revived interest in this area and many of the 'skeletons are now falling out of the closets.' For instance, from a book entitled *Black Settlers in Britain 1555—1958* by Nigel File and Chris Power is evidence that about twenty thousand black people were in London as early as 1764 working as servants though not as slaves.[2] A writer of that day made a complaint in *The Gentleman's Magazine* that Blacks were too many, considering that the population of London was only six hundred and seventy-six thousand, two hundred and twenty-five at that time. The writer further complained that the free negroes refused to put up with inequality, and to be forced to perform menial tasks.[3]

Another unpublished research made by Jos Williams, the Principal and Founder of Clearview College, Coventry, who came to Britain in the early sixties, claims that Black presence was prominent in Britain until the Anglo-Saxon invasions of the fifth and sixth centuries . . .'[4] The report also notes that there is

---

[1] *The Observer*, 4 October 1981.
[2] Nigel File and Chris Power, *Black Settlers in Britain 1555-1958* (Heinemann Educational Books Ltd., London 1981), p.1.
[3] *Ibid.*
[4] Jos Williams, *Research* (Clearview College of Further Education, Coventry n.d.)

evidence that since the sixteenth century Black people in England were serving as household servants in the English Courts as well as in the music business.

While some Black people in service to their wealthy masters were poorly treated and even marked like cattle, some serving the aristocrats were Christianized and given new names. They were dressed in fine clothes becoming to the status of their masters. Others, being cut off from their relations, fled from the homes of their keepers and often landed up in the poorer areas of the city. They were debarred from receiving poor relief and often fell foul of the law due to such circumstances. Crime such as prostitution, and other unlawful activities became their normal pre-occupation. For Blacks that were free, the condition was different as they were able to obtain jobs as labourers, dressmakers, street traders, tailors, musicians and entrepreneurs.[1] Some of the aristocracy took some interest in Black people in Britain at that time. The Duke of Montague is said to have shown much kindness to them. He introduced Francis Williams to Cambridge University, and was responsible for Job Ben Sullivan becoming a scholar in 1750.[2]

Another slave who benefited from the favour of some White masters was Francis Barber. He was born in Jamaica and brought to England by a ship's captain named Barthust in 1750. Barthust sent Francis to school at Barton in Yorkshire. After the death of Barthust, Francis who had earlier gained his freedom, went to serve Dr. Samuel Johnson (the man who became famous for making the English dictionary). Francis was later sent to school at Bishops Stortford, Hertfordshire, and, after the death of Dr Johnson in 1782, Francis inherited his property, an income of Seventy Pounds annually, and all his books. Francis married and moved to Lichfield with his wife Elizabeth and later established a school at Burntwood, near Lichfield. Elizabeth and Francis had four children, one of whom, Samuel, became a Methodist minister.[3]

In time, an active Black middle-class, though few in number, aligned themselves with the anti-slavery movement and provided leadership for the Black community. Famous Black writers like Ignatius Sancho, Ottobah Cugoana and Olaudah Equiano fraternized with high society and participated in political debates. It seemed that they approached the question of slavery differently to the popular abolitionist movements of their day. They rather fought the social system that was suppressing and exploiting all poor people.

It was in music and entertainment that Black people found an opportunity to move among the social classes and command a measure of self-respect. Londoners warmed toward their music, especially Turkish military music which was very popular at that time. The African Caribbean people, dressed in Turkish turbans, provided this entertainment. According to Jos Williams, in 1757 the British Army organized these Black musicians who became very popular and were always in demand at parades and festivities.[4]

---

[1] *Ibid.*
[2] *Ibid.*
[3] Nigel File and Charles Power, *Black Settlers in Britain 1555—1958*, p.2.
[4] Jos Williams, *Research.*

Between 1577 and 1833, Test Cases were presented in British courts in an attempt to define the legal status of slaves in Britain. While some decisions were quite sympathetic to the slaves, slavery was not outlawed. It took the untiring efforts of men like William Wilberforce, noted politician and philanthropist, and Sir Thomas Fowell Buxton, who in March 1823 presented a resolution in the House of Commons declaring that slavery was 'repugnant to the principles of the British Constitution and the Christian religion, and it ought to be gradually abolished throughout the British dominions.'[1] The Slavery Abolition Act they fought for was passed in 1833, one month before the death of Wilberforce.

After abolition, however, many Blacks did not have any change in status except that they were now free. Many remained in their position as domestic helpers and labourers. By the late nineteenth century the only jobs available to Black men were on the merchant ships. As jobs became scarce, men drifted from port to port in search of work. Cardiff attracted many Blacks because of the new port and flourishing coal industry in South Wales. The population of Blacks increased, and, when jobs later became scarce, discrimination against Black workers in favour of Whites forced many Blacks to live on the poverty line.

To foster racial solidarity, self-awareness, and total emancipation from white domination, the Pan-African Movement was founded and the first conference was held in London in 1900. The conference served notice that Black people throughout the Empire would one day be free from oppression to play their role in international affairs.

In 1931 the League of Coloured People was formed by Dr. Harold Moody. He was born in Jamaica but came to England in 1908 as a student at Kings's College Hospital in London. There, he excelled and specialized in ophthalmics. As a devout Christian, his concern for Blacks in Britain forced him to form this nation-wide group to champion the cause for equal rights and opportunity for Blacks. It served as a pressure group in the community and as a support mechanism during the war, in helping to provide accommodation for Blacks, and to resist the American practice of segregation against Black troops. Through Moody's efforts the Government was persuaded to alter its requirement that discriminated against Blacks holding senior ranks in the Army. It is significant that this move broke barriers for Blacks as Capt. Arundel Moody, son of Dr. Moody enlisted in the Royal West Kent Regiment, where he became the first Black to be commissioned as an officer in the British army. Further, in 1942 the LCP adopted the Charter of Coloured People at a meeting held at Manchester. This called for self-government in the Colonies and equal rights for Blacks in Britain.

During the Second World War, Black soldiers were welcomed, but when the war was over the old myths about Blacks again surfaced and African Caribbean troops were separated from their White wives and associates. Those who chose to remain in the country after being discharged from the Army found the attitude of the British, for whom they had fought, intolerable. However, there was some comfort in the fact that not all eyes were closed to the achievements of Black people in the war effort. Lord Moyne, then Secretary of State for the

---

[1] James M. Phillip, *Jamaica: Its Past and Present State* (Unwin Brother, London 1943), p.102.

Colonies, praised the work of Blacks in a speech in the House when he is reported to have observed:

'A great amount of valuable war work was being done by men of African descent in ways less prominent in the public eye. We had had hundreds of highly skilled technicians from West Indies and Africa, thousands of seamen who were continually facing the terrible dangers of sub-marines, hundreds from the West Indies who had come over to join the Royal Air Force.'[1]

(b) RUDE AWAKENING FOR NEW ARRIVALS

World War II was over and Britain was short of manpower. The British Government invited African Caribbeans and Asians to come to Britain to facilitate the labour shortage. London Transport advertised what seemed to the Caribbean people to be lucrative job opportunities, and hospitals offered ready admissions for those wishing to train as nurses for the Health Service. In the Caribbean, jobs were scarce and for many the prospect of going to Britain to work was an opportunity of a lifetime.

People of the Colonies were deeply committed to the British way of life and values, and the thought of coming to the motherland was the hope of a better life. A good number left whatever jobs they had, and the vast majority of the jobless and aspiring students, enthusiastically embarked on the long trek across the Atlantic seeking their own fortune. Many were ill prepared for the conditions that were awaiting them. As they had showered love, respect and hospitality on those who had visited their shores, they held the illusion that the same treatment would be returned in the motherland. As many were brought up in towns and villages where it was customary to greet people on the streets, and where most people went to church on Sundays, they unwittingly expected the same conditions existed in England.

Most of the new arrivals settled in London, Birmingham, and the industrial towns where jobs were readily available. Soon it became apparent that coping with the complex and unfriendly host society, and being subjected to racial discrimination and harassment, were situations many were ill-prepared to handle. In some areas of London in the late Fifties, attacks on Blacks were commonplace. Cries went out to 'keep Britain White', and some Members of Parliament (MP) argued for the repatriation of their colonial brothers who had fearlessly fought for this country in two world wars. Moreover, their presence in Britain was on the invitation to help in the post-war reconstruction. Ironically, Mr. Enoch Powell, who as Minister of Health (1960-1963) encouraged the recruiting of African Caribbeans to work in this country, turned around and championed the call for repatriation in 1968. He did not mince words in his notorious 'River of Blood' speech which was so racist that he was evicted from the Shadow Cabinet of the Conservative Party.

---

[1] Nigel and Power, p.45.

Some news media with their emotive reports added more fuel to the kindling fires of racial strife. It was no surprise that race riots erupted in Notting Hill, London, and the police hostility to the Black community began to surface. Hope now gone, it was left to the Black communities to form their own social groupings for their own protection.

It is the opinion of some that the Government of that day was caught in a dilemma and unable to contain the situation by taking action on behalf of the persecuted minorities. Instead, it passed the 1962 Commonwealth Immigration Act which was intended to limit immigration into Britain as a means of dealing with the problem. As years went by more restrictive measures were enacted, culminating in the Nationality Act of 1981 which openly legislated against all non-white Commonwealth peoples, and limit their opportunity for British Citizenship. The only positive action taken to ease the lot of the non-white Commonwealth people were the Race Relations Act of the 1965, 1968 and 1976. These Acts, though intended to make discrimination against Blacks an offence, were impotent in the face of the latent and covert institutional racism of the British society. More importantly, with the Single European Act of 1992, Blacks feel even more threatened, as the other European countries do not have any race relation laws as in Britain. These fears were clearly outlined by Black leaders at a meeting at the Home office called to discuss these issues.

(c) HOPE THROUGH THE CHURCH

The emergence of the New Testament Church of God (NTCG) in Britain was a direct result of the large number of its members among the migrants who flocked to Britain seeking a better life. Exciting stories have been related of their many and varied experiences encountered during their long and tiring journey from the Islands to Britain. For those who had never travelled beyond the confines of their village markets, the challenge of the voyage across the wide Atlantic, the uncomfortable train journey across Italy, Switzerland and France to Calais, and across the English Channel to Dover were traumatic experiences that many have never forgotten. Some travelled other routes or by air, while a minority came on the famous banana boats.

Among the emigrés were pastors who for the first time were exposed to the harsh expression of riotous and licentious living on boats, and so they made no delay in registering their evangelistic concerns for the souls of their shipmates. Many preached and prayed for them that they should not forget God in their search for riches and pleasure. On arrival in Britain too, many sought to find places of worship but were rudely shocked by the attitude of the English people to religion as a whole, and to church attendance on Sunday in particular. Some even experienced racial discrimination and rejection when they sought to worship at the mainline churches whose missionaries served in their homelands.

Some of these early leaders, such as Rev. Dr. O. A. Lyseight, G. S. Peddie and L. Monfries (both deceased), H. D. Brown and G. A. Johnson ministered in indigenous Pentecostal and Independent Churches in their areas from time to time. While their hosts were happy to have them come sometimes, it seemed that a permanent relationship was not much desired, as the newcomers seemed to be too noisy, and, in the eyes of the newcomers, the worship was not as inspiring as that they were used to 'back home.'

Sensing a wider need within the growing Black community for fellowship away from home, and realizing that many of their friends were falling prey to the spiritual inertia that was rampant everywhere, these leaders embarked upon a militant plan to establish a fellowship to preserve their spiritual life until they could return to the Caribbean. Many of them had no intentions of remaining in Britain for more than about five years, especially those who faced hostility and severe hardship in finding adequate housing. Often, as they searched for accommodation to let, they came across signs in shop windows which read, 'NO IRISH, NO NIGGERS, NO DOGS'. Some Blacks did not help the situation either, for if they were fortunate to obtain a large room or purchase a house, they sublet it at an exorbitant rate. Some workers could only rent a space on a bed for the night or day, depending on what shift they worked. Men who were fortunate to have their wives or girl friends with them occupied their one room as bedroom, kitchen and dining room. When children were born, they shared the same accommodation with their parents as they could seldom afford two rooms due to their meagre wages.

Such conditions created much despair, and some African Caribbean people who had left good jobs at home could not cope with the frustrations. Some actually lost hope and became mentally ill and were committed to institutions, or repatriated. Others sought for the Church as the only place of refuge as they were cut off from loved ones and hopelessly trapped in situations and systems that were unfamiliar and obscure.

The evangelistic fervour of the members of the Church burned high and soon groups of believers were formed in homes and school rooms in many parts of the country. It was quite evident that those who had a firm faith in God managed to endure the conditions more favourably. For them, their God was alive and responding to their prayers. For others, however, the conditions were too grievous. They lost faith in God and the Church, and sought help in their own way.

The first public service held by some NTCG members was in September 1953 at the YMCA Hall, Waterloo Road, Wolverhampton, in the West Midlands, under the direction of O. A. Lyseight and H. D. Brown. When the Church was later organized with twenty-five members, three White British families were included. About the same time, G. A. Johnson, Enos Gordon, and other believers began a fellowship in Handsworth, Birmingham. Contact was made between the Wolverhampton group and the Handsworth group, and O. A. Lyseight often visited Handsworth to minister to that group. It must be borne in mind that O. A. Lyseight and J. A. Johnson were ministers of the New Testament Church of God in Jamaica before coming to England.

In time, both groups at Wolverhampton and Handsworth were officially recognized by general leaders of the Church of God with international offices in Cleveland, Tennessee, USA, and O. A. Lyseight was set as the National Overseer, a position he held for twenty-four years.

The starting of the Church in the London area was similarly born out of a felt need among immigrant members of the NTCG to maintain a sound spiritual standard of living in what they saw as a very loose and permissive society. One young man with a deep burden over the condition was James Tomlin from the New Testament Church of God at Bombay, Manchester, Jamaica. He arrived in London in May of 1955. Conscious of the spiritual hunger among friends in his area, he wrote back to a friend and minister in Jamaica urging him to come to England to start a Church. He rented a church hall in preparation for the coming of his friend, and in October of that same year, the Reverend S.U. Thompson, leaving his wife and young family in Jamaica, arrived in London.

Unfortunately he became ill on arrival and was not able to attend the first meeting of the group. He recalls that the meeting was held at the St. Stephens Parish Hall, Dorset Road, Oval, London SW9. However, the group soon moved to St. Paul's Church hall at Alladice Street, Brixton. In those days, the support of the Church of England parish priests and other church leaders in assisting NTCG local branches in finding suitable places where they could house their followers was invaluable.[1] Other ministers and members who found occasional fellowship in other organizations often visited the Brixton group. Among these were Reverend E. Swaby and Mother E. Beccan, a lay preacher at that time. Before long, Swaby was encouraged to start a prayer meeting in his home in Kilburn, N.W. London, and out of that a Church was formed at Kilburn. One of the first converts to join this fellowship was C. L. Hastings who was converted in the Billy Graham Crusade in London in June of 1955. Hastings who trained as a Research Engineer, was later to become a leader, pioneering Churches in Reading, and Slough, and working in setting up Sunday Schools in Letchworth and Aldershot.

The Brixton Church became a focus for revival under the dynamic leadership of S. U. Thompson and soon a branch was formed at Croydon when the late Peter Barrett came to England. He found a former believer from Jamaica, Mercedes Amos, and prayer meetings were started in her home. Other believers living in the area soon found a meeting place and a new Church was on its way.

In 1961, the Church at Brixton purchased a building at Offley Road, Oval, and began to experience rapid growth. Soon the building became too small for the congregation, and the pastor began tithing members (i.e. giving one tenth of them away) to start new groups in different areas. This pattern of growth led to the development of Churches at Catford, Clapham and Deptford.

As mentioned earlier, the group that formed the Church in Kilburn was started by prayer meetings at Pastor Swaby's home. They moved to a Scout hall on Kilburn High Road, but after a few weeks, had to move to another Scout Hall at Greyhound Road. There, they experienced some of the racial harrassment that was not uncommon in those days, as White youngsters took pleasure in stoning

---

[1] This support continues till this day and has been found to be extremely helpful both to the host Church and the NTCG congregations.

the building while they worshipped. However, this was soon brought under control. The Church remained there and grew as believers, especially from Jamaica, were attracted to this place for worship.

When a pastor was later found for the Kilburn group in the person of E. G. Cummings, Pastor Swaby began pioneering a Church in Deptford, while Mother Beccan spent her time assisting in the development of a work with some Polish brethren at Marble Arch. However, Pastor Swaby still held the position of District Pastor for the newly developing Kilburn District.

In time, Reverend E. G. Kellywright who was assisting in the Church at Stoke Newington, was appointed to replace Cummings as pastor at Kilburn. He and his congregation purchased a redundant, and dilapidated Methodist Church building at Willesden High Road, in 1964. The brethren lovingly and enthusiastically set about to redeem the building from destruction, and demonstrated that they had brought with them skills of the trade from the Caribbean.

Then followed over the years, a series of changes in the pastorate in which ministers such as R. Kennedy, K. Peterkin and I. Brooks made their unique contributions to the Church's growth and development. In 1986, the Reverend I. Lewinson was transferred to this pastorate and the Church continues to enjoy increase in spite of the retirement of some members back to the Caribbean, and the regression of others who find the way too straight and narrow.

The Church at Deptford was started with ten members from the Oval group, in a Sunday School Hall which was later burned down. When the Rev. Ferdinand Hylton, himself a veteran of the faith, took over the pastorate, he purchased a church building there and pastored it for seventeen years. Now there is in Deptford a flourishing Church under the leadership of the Rev. H. Strachan.

The work of pioneer, Pastor E. Beccan, was not confined to that among the Polish brethren; she was a fervent and hard worker, assisting wherever she was called upon to serve. Her greatest contribution was in the development of the Church at Mile End where a neatly built chapel now stands at Grove Lane, much to her credit. This church is now being pastored by the Rev. Joel Edwards, under whose uniquely charismatic leadership, it has experienced tremendous growth in that Inner City area, over the last two years.

As was the experience of several young men who came to this country seeking work but later took up the ministry, James Tomlin was to become a pioneering minister. A prayer group was started in the home of Mother Letts who lived in Catford, but attended the Oval Church. As it developed, James Tomlin was made the pastor. The Church grew rapidly, and when Pastor Tomlin left to return to Jamaica, the Rev. D. Miller was sent there as pastor. Some years later, a redundant Methodist church building was bought at Lee High Road, London S.E. 12. Pastor Miller served successfully until his retirement in January, 1987. At present, this Church is still experiencing good growth under the leadership of the Rev. U. L. Simpson, formerly pastor at Aldershot, home of the British Army.

Over in Stoke Newington, North London, a group of believers under the leadership of Reverend C. Marsh began meeting at the Town Hall in 1957. Before long, Marsh and his followers joined the New Testament Church of God, and moved to the Bouverie Road Scout Hall for worship. Once per week, the young fellowship met at the the Congregational Church hall at Tottenham, for their Youth meetings. The Rev. Dr. Clifford Hill was the minister at that time.

By 1963, there was a division in the group and the members who remained faithful to the NTCG purchased a redundant Congregational Church building at Cricketfield Road and Downs Park Road, Clapton, and moved there. Among the early leaders of the Stoke Newington group were V. R. N Nelson, E. G. Kellywright, Arnold Williams, I. N. Carter, A. M. Scott, S. E. Arnold, F. Hosang, M. Brown, J. Arnold (née Scott), O. Paris, and others.

The first National Convention of the young and fledgling NTCG was held at the Villa Road Methodist Church, Handsworth, Birmingham. The meetings challenged the members to undertake the task of spreading the gospel in Britain as they perceived the country to be ripe for harvesting. S. U. Thompson was one of the speakers at that meeting. He took a photograph in front of the building and sent it home to his family. One of the children, on seeing the picture remarked, 'Daddy is becoming a white man!' Ironically, the Rev. S. U. Thompson is now pastor of this Church where he has served for twenty-four years. This was the first building to be purchased by the young organization in 1963, when G. A. Johnson was the pastor, and it also became, for many years, the national offices and Convention arena for the general Church.

The formation of the NTCG in the North of England had three separate streams. Immigrant believers who sought work in the cities of the then flourishing steel and textile industries soon found that they too needed the Church to succour them from the cold. In 1956, F. F. Poyser, a young minister from Jamaica, gathered six other believers in a kitchen of an immigrant home off Granville Road, Sheffield, and laid the foundation for what has now become our third largest church in the nation, now being led by the Reverend Benjamin Grey.

About the same time, Curtis Grey, a young man working on the buses, felt a deep call of God to start a group in Leeds. He, along with Isaiah Campbell, started a fellowship at his home at 43 Louis Street and the Church was organized on 14 May 1959. Brother Blair, one of the first converts, is a deacon of the Church today. Grey also pioneered Churches in Bradford, Huddersfield, Halifax, and campaigned in Newcastle-upon-Tyne where the Gospel tent was burned down. The Church in Leeds now under the leadership of Rev. C. L. Hastings has grown to be the fourth largest NTCG in the nation.

About 1965, C. Grey was transferred to pastor the Wolverhampton Church, in West Midlands. His evangelistic zeal led him to organize Churches in Stafford, Redditch, Wellinghall, and Cardiff, South Wales. Grey was sent to Liberia as a Missionary in 1973 and he is now Missionary Overseer in Nigeria where he has already served seven years and the Church has experienced extensive growth.

The third stream to join the NTCG was the Manchester group which began in the bedsit of Mary Jane Higgins who came to England in 1956. Finding no suitable place to worship in the Moss Side area where most African Caribbeans were settling at that time, Evangelist Higgins began to hold prayer meetings in her home. She was assisted by Brother and Sister S. Nembhard, Brother and Sister L. Ricketts, Brother McCrae and others who also held prayer meetings in their homes.

Sister Nembhard, desiring to see the church established, wrote to the general headquarters of the Church of God at Cleveland, Tennessee, USA requesting help. She was directed to contact the Rev. O. A. Lyseight who was the Overseer of the Church in England, and residing at Wolverhampton. Up until that time, the Manchester group did not know of the existence of the NTCG. The Rev. O. A. Lyseight, upon receiving the call from Manchester, visited the group taking along the Rev. G. A. Johnson, the Rev. Elisha Tennant and Brother Humphrey.

Concerned that the Church would not progress in the limited space in a bed-sit, Sister Nembhard succeeded in renting the Webster Street School Hall from the Council for one pound and twenty pence per week for Sunday worship. The group then voted to have a leader and the Rev. O. A. Lyseight appointed Evangelist Victoria Nelson from Birmingham to be the official leader.

Unfortunately, her tenure was not to last long as quarrels among them did not permit her to exercise her office. She had to throw in the towel and return to Birmingham.

The Rev. O. A. Lyseight returned to Manchester in an effort to restore fellowship and organized a tent meeting at Fairlawn Street. He also appointed Jeremiah McIntyre from Balsall Heath, Birmingham, as the pastor towards the end of 1959. The Rev. Jeremiah McIntyre commuted from Birmingham to Manchester for several months until he was able to move there to reside and established the Church in 1960 with 10 members. Under his leadership it grew rapidly, even though some of the pioneer members had left to form groups of their own. Through the leadership of Jeremiah McIntyre Churches were also organized at Crewe, Preston, Bolton, Oldham and Southampton. Some evangelistic efforts were also made in Liverpool and Cheetham Hill, Manchester, but no groups were organized.

After the Rev. Jeremiah McIntyre was transferred to London in 1967, the Rev. Glenford Elijah Hutchinson was appointed pastor. He and his wife led the church for twelve years making tremendous gains. It is reported that 209 new members were added to the Church during their tenure. They left the pastorate to minister in the USA, in 1979. They were succeeded by the Rev. T. E. Caine who now pastors the Church which, under his dynamic leadership, has grown to be the second largest branch of the NTCG in England and Wales.

As members of the NTCG were scattered mainly in the inner cities and industrial areas, many began house Fellowships which eventually joined the main body. This pattern of evangelism was open to all, but particularly aimed at the swelling immigrant population, and proved to be very successful. Within thirty-seven years, the Church has spread to twenty-five counties with a baptized membership of over seven thousand, and a constituency of over eighteen thousand (Appendix 1).

This brief review of the Church is not presumed to be the chronological and historical account of its development in Britain but is rather a sketch of the early beginnings for the purpose of this work. It is by no means comprehensive.

The Church became the centre for worship, fellowship and ministry to a growing number of people who were otherwise uncared for in the society. Most services were conducted in an atmosphere of lively and soul-stirring singing and hand-clapping, often followed by congregational praying and sometimes, speaking in tongues by the inspiration of the Holy Spirit. Miraculous healings were sometimes experienced through the prayer of faith. The Bible was central to the worship and most members were expected to bring their Bibles to Church and participate in Bible reading. Believers found comfort in the fact that their trials of life were only temporary, and some day they would lay their burdens down.' A typical song assured one that:

My trials here on earth will cease,
Some day, some day;
And I will have unending peace,

Some day, some day.

No more in darkness I will roam,
Some day, some day;
But rest eternally at home,
Some day, some day. (J. Graydon Hall).

To those who feel denied of earthly comforts, or perceive that the ungodly seem to be having all their heart's desire while their needs remain unmet, the consolation for the committed believer was in knowing that 'Jesus is all I need.'

Some have argued that the Church was just a palliative for a people under stress in a hostile and unfriendly society. But for those who were deeply committed to the faith, it offered everlasting hope. They would endorse the words of Paul:

'Therefore, since we have been justified through faith, we have peace with God through our Lord Jesus Christ, through whom we have gained access by faith into this grace in which we now stand. And we rejoice in the hope of the glory of God. Not only so, but we also rejoice in suffering, because we know that suffering produces perseverance; perseverance character; and character, hope. And hope does not disappoint us, because God has poured out his love into our hearts by the Holy Spirit, whom he has given us.' (Rom. 5.1-5 NIV).

It has often been argued that the New Testament Church of God and other Black-led churches were formed in this country because of the racism that the Black community experienced from host Churches. While the racism and rejection of some mainline Churches may have added opportunity for the spread of the movement, it must be clearly understood that most of these Black-led Churches and the New Testament Church of God in particular, were branches of organizations already existing in other parts of the world. The NTCG is an integral part of the Church of God which is established in over one hundred and sixteen countries of the world. The Church is also established in fourteen countries of Europe. The fact that the membership is mainly Black in the UK is because those who established the Church were immigrant families from the Caribbean.

The NTCG has been branded as a 'Black Church' or Black people's church. The truth is, the foundation faith of most of the Caribbean people was laid by Western missionaries who came to the colonies hundreds of years ago. In most cases the religious heritage of the Caribbean people was mainly British. Pentecostalism and its accompanying gifts were introduced from American in the early twentieth century.

The first New Testament Church of God was formed in the Bahamas in 1910. Edmond S. Barr, a native (Black) from the Bahama Islands, while residing in Pleasant Grove, Florida, attended an evangelistic meeting where he and his wife Rebecca received the Baptism of the Holy Ghost. He had a deep desire to return to his home country to share the news of his new-found faith. A retired Methodist preacher, R. M. Evans who had earlier received this experience, raised the money to assist Barr to return to the Bahamas.

In 1910, Evans and his wife and Carl M. Padgett arrived in Nassau, and soon located Barr. He then wrote back to the Church in the U.S.A. stating that he had found Brother and Sister Barr, making full proof of their ministry. In the words of Evans,
'... although the usual places of worship were as a rule, closed to them, yet they had rented a hall, and were faithfully preaching all phases of the full gospel of Christ including the baptism of the Holy Ghost, as indicated by the Bible sign of speaking in tongues ... And the Spirit was already moving upon the hearts of the people.'[1]

From this record it clearly indicates that Edmond Barr, an African Caribbean, became the first man to take the Church of God message outside continen-tal USA.

In 1917, the Church of God added to its organization four Churches and eighty members in Jamaica. These Churches were under the leadership of F. L. Ryder, a Barbadian (Black) from Bridgetown, Barbados.[2] In 1924 when an American, E. E. Simmons was sent to Jamaica as Overseer, he could not find any of these Churches and so he began a new work and by 1925, four new Churches were organized. That laid the foundation of what is now the NTCG with over 36,000 members in the Island.

It can therefore, be clearly seen that the New Testament Church of God did not just spring up in the United Kingdom as a result of rejection; it was a divinely led mission to this land. The members and leaders of this Church on arrival in Britain saw the necessity, as responsible Christians, to sound the clarion call to the people at large to heed the gospel of the Lord Jesus Christ. Recognizing that Britain, once the bastion of Christianity, was now a post-Christian society, and greatly secularized, the Church strove to point people to the better life in Christ. They understood that this new life could only be attained as one identified with Christ and the blessed hope of his soon return, and his Kingdom.

---

[1] Charles W. Conn, *Like A Mighty Army* (Church of God Pub. House, Tennessee 1955), p.113.
[2] *Ibid.* p.144.

(d) A NEW GENERATION IN A NEW AGE

As previously stated, the NTCG in Great Britain was established in 1953 when immigrants from the Caribbean came to this country in search of a better life. Most all of them would agree that their intentions were to work, or train and return home after a few years. However, as conditions for some became better they stayed on and thus became the nucleus of the new Church. Some, unfortunately, did not find that better life and became trapped in a system from which they could find no escape. They could neither go home, nor enjoy any economic success, as they had envisioned when they left home. For such, the Church has been their only consolation as they live in hope for a day when their 'change will come.'

After three decades of existence in the United Kingdom, the Church now finds that there are four categories of people within its membership:

1. those who came from the Caribbean as members and those who were acquainted with the Church in the Caribbean and became members here;
2. the children of both categories who were born in the Caribbean, brought to the UK at a tender age, or who were born and educated here;
3. the grand-children of Group 1 and children of Group 2;
4. those who were totally new to the church.

It is to the third group that I refer as the new generation in a new age. This generation of adults and youngsters have little in common with their parents' or grandparents' traditions. In very many respects, some seem to have little understanding of their parents' desperate struggle for survival in this country, and how it affected them. Most African Caribbean people who came to this country were deeply religious, even though many did not maintain the piety that they understood their religion demanded. They were brought up to respect or reverence the things of God and the Church. To find oneself in the church on Sunday was a duty not to be ignored. To strive to obey the Ten Commandments, especially, with regard to loving one's neighbour was a goal of life. It was no wonder that they were rudely awakened to the fact that in the towns and cities of the UK one did not, as a rule greet another on the streets, unless one was acquainted with that individual. For most people, life in Britain was fast becoming another type of slavery from which they thought they had escaped. One soon learnt that one's whole life revolved around one's job, with no time for worship or leisure, for enough money was to be earned to support the family left behind in the Caribbean and the family developing in Britain.

Children born during such bitter struggles were often brought up by babysitters in whose one-room accommodation—sometimes damp and cramped—there was no space to play. They never understood why they were left there all day, just bundled up in a crib or pram, and picked up in the evenings when their parents took them home to another room just as cramped.

Today, some children are privileged to be nursed at creches or day nurseries. Such facilities were too difficult to find in those days, nor could parents afford them if they were available.

But in spite of all those depressing conditions, believing parents exercised faith in God to see them through. Their faith was undergirded when they went to Church and worshipped God.

In their pursuit of a better life and struggle to own their own homes, many parents neglected to see that their children had been given proper education. In the Caribbean, the teachers looked after the welfare of children. As a result many Caribbean parents were under the false impression that the same system would obtain in Britain. After all, this country was the fountain head of learning and knowledge.

Some parents too, seldom asked how their children were progressing at school, or whether they had homework to be done. As a matter of fact, with Dad doing constant night work and Mum on an early shift, the children hardly had time with their parents. Some, who were fortunate, depended on the television for comfort. A majority of Black children have grown up being alien to their parents. At school, they faced severe trauma. Racial discrimination and rejection soon became apparent, and, to worsen the situation, there was no support structure in the home. I had an informal discussion with a group of young people recently, and one explained how she was faced with racial abuse at the age of five. Some said they could not report such things at home for their parents were either too busy to listen or would blame them for misbehaving. The result was that a generation of youths grew up disillusioned both with their parents and the system in which they found themselves. They felt rejected and misunderstood both at home and in the society.

For some first generation parents of the NTCG in Britain, the pressures of life were mainly due to the evils of a sinful society. They endured the discrimination and racist taunts levelled against them. They were taught to 'pray for those who despitefully use you'; to 'turn the other cheek.' They cared not for the personal attack and abuse; they saw it as part of their cross bearing and suffering for the Name of Christ. They were taught that the Christian must be patient and submissive. To fight back was to give place to the devil. One of our pastor's sons was sent home with a note that he had been fighting at school. The pastor on ordering his son to account for his devious behaviour had this reply: 'Dad, the boy hit me, and remembering what you preach, I turned the other cheek. He hit me again, and since I did not have another cheek, I hit him back.' To John, that was the only way to handle what he felt was an untenable situation.

The non-violent passivism of the older generation has been lost as this new generation struggles to forge their own identity in Britain. Their parents were not brought up in a society with pressures of colour prejudice, rejection and ostracism. Unlike Black America, which—until the Civil Rights Bill of 1963,—had no freedom from oppression and racial discrimination, the African Caribbean had enjoyed freedom from racial discrimination and subjugation. However, they were held captive by colonialism which limited their opportunities for upward mobility in the face of the booming industrial revolution. Some were made fodder for the machinery that propelled wealth to the colonial masters, while others, who were favoured, selfishly relished the crumbs that fell from their masters' tables.

For the believers too, there was a protectionism that swelled from the fact that they mostly came from rural communities where everyone was one's keeper. Their home environment and social orientation were entirely different; hence the language and terms of reference were quite alien to that of their children now in Britain.

The new generation openly admit that there are conflicts between them and their parents. In discussions, some of the suggested factors were:

1. Lack of identity with their parents
2. Difference in up-bringing
3. Difference in culture
4. Confusion arising from attempts to mix the external influences with those in the home
5. Difference in traditions.

One youngster succinctly declared, 'Part of them is in us and we learn certain things from them; but we are different'.

One of the major complaints of the youths was the lack of tolerance on the part of their parents to the changes that have occurred in society, and their indifference to respond to the changing times. They noted that their parents were not prepared to accept the dress standards of the day, and their attitudes were too radical. They felt that their parents have allowed traditions and beliefs held from 'back home' to take precedence over proper Biblical exegesis.

This new generation also refuses to be docile with regard to matters that affect their relationships in the Church and society. They felt that when they spoke out, they were often regarded by their seniors as being too forward and rebellious. This they regarded as a failure on the part of the Church and their leaders to recognize them as worthy and important segments of the organization. Some did not wish to sever connections with the Church; they only wanted to be a part, working for a change that they saw as inevitable.

It may be helpful here to quote part of a letter I received from a member of one of our Churches which clearly sets out the feelings of some of the youth:

'Dear Overseer Arnold:

Greetings in the precious name of Jesus our soon coming King!

I feel compelled to write this letter and I pray that the contents will be noted and the points mentioned will be put into practice. I write this letter with deepest concern for us as young people and for the church in general, so don't misunderstand me in any way.

I am twenty-six years old and I have been a Christian since I was nine. The Lord has been and is good to me and I thank him for his blessings towards me. I am glad to know the Lord from my youth. I have found that, although the church provides for our spiritual being, our church is seriously failing to provide adequately for our social, physical, and emotional needs. It grieves me to hear of so many people, particularly young people, leaving the Church. I find in many cases that, especially young converts, the Word of God alone will not sustain them. One cannot say that if they were grounded in the Lord they would not have back-slidden as I have often heard it said. We (the church) should show that we care for all areas of their lives . . . .'

It would appear to the average reader from such impassioned sentiments as expressed in this letter that the NTCG has not made room for any activities other than spiritual ones. On the contrary, there is a department of Youth and Christian Education that conducts camps, seminars, conventions, talent competitions, and play schemes etc., which are designed to cater for all the needs of our youth socially, as well as, spiritually. There is also a department of Ladies Ministries that specializes in programmes to meet the needs of the women and young ladies of the Church. For some youths, however, rightly or wrongly, there are other social involvements that have been grossly neglected or overlooked. This underscores the urgency for action on the part of Church leaders carefully to consider the needs of this new generation.

2. Searching for Roots

(a) NATIONAL HEADQUARTERS—OVERSTONE

Discreetly tucked away amidst luscious trees and thirty-two acres of rolling parkland is the beautiful Victorian Manor that now houses the National Headquarters of the New Testament Church of God, and its Theological Institution, in Overstone Park, Northampton. Bill Bosworth writing in *Northants and Bedford Life,* July 1975, states, Northampton is popularly known as the county of spires, squires and shires and an area which typifies this aspect of the county is Overstone.' The previous owners of the property were the Overstone School for Girls, Lady Wantage and the Lord Overstone , for whom the building was first built. A report in *The Northampton Independent* reads:

'. . . The fine mansion and estate of Overstone Park has been acquired by Sir Philip Stott, the famous architect and engineer of the Stanton Court, Worcester, and presented to the Conservative Party as a Summer School for Conservative political students . . .. The college is primarily intended to benefit the working men and women of the Party, who lack the facilities for past school education, but all members of the Party are entitled to apply for enrolment as students and it is hoped that members of Parliament, candidates, and others will attend. The accommodation for students is on a most complete and convenient scale, with full facilities for sports, boating, fishing etc., after study hours. The latter, which consists of the mornings and one hour in the evenings only, are occupied with lectures and debates etc., on all matters relating to constitutional history and political economy.'[1]

The building as it now stands was built during 1860-1864 and was designed by W.A.Teulon. As mentioned above, the property was formerly owned by Lady Wantage, daughter of Lord Overstone. Lord Wantage was a famous landlord and philanthropist through whose generosity the Abington Park was donated to the Northampton people.

In 1929, the building was occupied by the Overstone Girls School when it was acquired by Henrietta Franklyn. The School ran for fifty years as a private residential college with students paying over two thousand pounds per year. The decision to close the school was, for the students, a very disastrous one. One of the head pupils on that fateful day summed up the feelings of all the students when she remarked:

'It's very upsetting for all of us. Overstone is a fantastic building and there's always been a good friendly atmosphere here between the staff and the girls. I'm going to miss it dreadfully.'[2]

The then headmaster, Colonel Peter Clarke, is reported to have conceded that the high cost of repair estimated at £250,000 was beyond the ability of the school to raise at that time and so there was no alternative but to sell. Nine months later,

---

[1] 'Students in Residence at Overstone' (*The Northampton Independent,* 5 May 1923).
[2] 'Breaking those Old School Ties' in *Chronicle & Echo* 27 May 1980.

my predecessor the Rev. J. McIntyre came along and purchased the Manor which houses 116 rooms on a 32-acre plot, along with the Henrietta Franklyn Hall for over £140,000, and stated that the property would serve '. . . as our main training centre in the country, and we are going to be selective as to who comes to Overstone as the standard of the centre will depend on the quality of people attending.'[1]

And so it happened that, in these famous Halls, this African Caribbean Church pitched its camp. Perhaps, if there were ghosts, they might have been running around wondering what has gone wrong with the world. But here we are training students for the ministry, and administering some 107 congregations and missions spread over the country. The Churches are mainly located in areas where there have been large populations of ethnic people, and mainly in the inner cities (See Appendix I). The Church, though open to all, became the centre for social interaction, and caring concern for the disadvantaged large populations of ethnic people, many of whom lived mainly in the Inner Cities.

(b) NATIONAL OVERSEER

The National Overseer (Bishop) is the executive head of the organization with an Episcopal form of Government. The area is divided up into Districts of which there are twenty-two throughout England and Wales, each headed by a District Overseer. The highest governing body in the organization is the National Executive Council, and the National Overseer serves as Chairman. His duties are, executive, supervisory, administrative, promotional, and disciplinary. His appointment is for a four-year term which is renewable biennially at the behest of the World Missions Board, Cleveland, Tennessee, USA which is the appointing body. There is no limitation on the number of years the Overseer in England may serve.

Before coming to this office, I served as pioneer missionary Overseer to Ghana, West Africa, from 1966-1976. I was then posted to Nigeria, West Africa, where I also served as missionary Overseer from 1976-1984. I assumed the office of Overseer in the United Kingdom in August 1984.

Born the last child of a family of eleven children, I was brought up in the strict traditions of the early Methodists. Following a deeper commitment to Christ and my belief in water baptism by immersion, I was forced to seek this experience and later became a member of a young group of believers in Trinidad called the Christian General Assembly. This was in 1953. I later received the Baptism of the Holy Spirit and was called to preach. Our group joined the New Testament Church of God in 1955. Much of my ministry has been in the areas of preaching, teaching, and administration. I served as National Youth Director of the NTCG in the UK from 1960 to 1961 and then became National Youth and Christian Education Director from 1961 to 1966. I also held the position of National Secretary/Treasurer from 1963 to 1966.

During this time, I also served as Dean of Students of the Ebenezer Bible Institute, Handsworth, Birmingham. EBI was the first theological institution— as far as I am aware—to be started by a Black-led Church in this country.

---

[1] 'Nothing to Fear' in *Chronicle & Echo* 27 May 1980.

After two decades of stimulating growth and progress the NTCG found that it was losing a grip on its younger generation. For the purpose of this study a group made up of mainly second generation NTCG members drawn from around the nation was formed. This group was called a Site Team, the churches in the nation becoming the site of our investigation. It was felt that this was the only way in which the issues that were affecting the youth of the Church could be properly researched and expressed. The task was then to select from around the nation suitably placed persons who could find the time and enthusiasm for such an undertaking. Some were contacted by telephone and others were written to. Finally, the following persons consented to be a part of the programme that was to lead us down avenues we had never dreamed of exploring before. The members were as follows:

Gwendolyn Morrison is a Nursing Sister. She is from Trinidad and came to England in 1957 while quite young. She is married to a Jamaican and they have a daughter and two sons. Gwendolyn is a very committed Christian; active in church work, especially in Women's ministries. She has a peculiar sense of humour and added a lot of life to our meetings. At her Church in Clapton, her husband faithfully serves as one of the local officers.

Cynthia Spence is the daughter of one of our lady preachers. She works as an housing officer and is married to a goldsmith, Vernon Spence. They are a very lovely couple who are devoted to the Lord and the Church. Cynthia serves in the ladies department of her local church at Handsworth, Birmingham. She also teaches Sunday School, and was once the National Teen Soloist of the year. She was also a founding member of the famous Gospel group called 'Majestics'. Along with her group she toured the Continent, Scotland and the USA in the Seventies. She is a lifeline in her local church's social responsibility projects. Cynthia has a very winsome personality and is very hospitable. She and her husband are the proud parents of three sons and one daughter.

Velma Dean, at the time of the research, was my Secretary and did some typing for the Site Team and the project. She is from London and moved to Northampton in 1982 to work as Secretary to the previous Overseer. Velma strongly represented the views of the younger generation of the Church having joined the NTCG in England and was totally ignorant of the back home' traditions and church culture. She hoped that lots of changes in the way the Church was run would have taken place by the time the project was completed and was therefore happy to make her contribution.

One who had taken a very active role in the project, both behind the scenes and at the Site Team meetings was my wife, *Joyce Arnold*. She was very helpful in the selection of the members of the Site Team. As one who has been very active in the Church as Youth leader, Women's President, preacher, teacher and minister's wife, she has a burden for the progress of the NTCG and shares a deep concern for the youth. We have laboured together and carried the load of leadership for the past twenty-nine years and in this project she articulated a similar concern for something new to happen that might give stability and direction to the Church. There is only one love that has overtaken her interest and that is for our son, now twelve years old, for whom we waited seventeen years of our marriage.

Colin Mitchell is the Jew with whom we took our journey. He got converted due to the fact that a Black female member of our Church who worked in his office lived out her Christian testimony. He accepted her invitation to attend church and became convicted of his need for inner peace. He could not resist the appeal to seek Jesus Christ as Saviour and so he surrendered his life to the claims of Christ. Later, while studying at our Bible Institute in London, he fell in love with another Black Christian and married her. They have two lovely children, Ben, seven years and Sophi, four. Colin is a Social Worker and Licensed Exhorter in the NTCG. He loves to preach and witness of the love of Jesus Christ. He is one Jew that has a lovely sense of humour and a passionate desire to see the church making an impact on the British society. As a Social Worker, he is conscious of the frustration and hopelessness of many black youths in East London where he lives and works. He made a tremendous contribution to the Site Team process.

Andrew Moore, Ia financial Accountant and also a Licensed Minister within the NTCG is from Luton. A Caucasian British, he was selected to help in the understanding of the ways in which the Church was perceived by the White community. Andrew is married with three sons. He and his wife were Jehovah's Witnesses before their conversion to Christ. He explained that after years of working as a Jehovah's Witness, he found the Lord through the witness of a Jamaican lady. Andrew worked with the Site Team in the initial stages but found it difficult after a while to attend Site Team meetings. He had promised his wife that he would spend Saturdays at home with the children since he was out all week. This commitment he found difficult to defer in favour of the continued work on the Site Team. Because of the nature of the work of most members, we could not meet otherwise than on Saturdays, and had to reluctantly release Andrew from the Team.

Representing the Youth department of our Church on the Site Team was *Eric Brown*, an ordained Minister of the NTCG. He was working in the Housing Department at Hackney, London where he was exposed to all the poverty and squalor of that area of the Inner City, when he was called to do full-time service for the Church. Eric and his wife Millicent have three lovely boys. He had only moved to Northampton one year before the project began. As National Director of Youth and Christian Education of the NTCG, Eric sensed an urgent need for the Church to come to grips with the problems of social responsibility. Having been brought up in the Church in Jamaica, he could relate to the vision and understanding of the older members. However, he did his college training in London and was fully conversant with the problems that Blacks and ethnic youths experience in the schools and colleges. Eric serves on the National Parole Board, Race Relations Board and as General Secretary for the African West Indian United Council of Churches (AWUCOC). He has travelled widely in the interest of the Church.

Another member of the Site Team who by his work and ministry had been dealing with the youth of the Church was *Rudolph Parkinson*. He served as National Youth and Christian Education Director for eight years (1975-1983). Rudolph and his wife Cherry have two daughters. As National Secretary of the NTCG, a position he has held since 1985, he is at the place to assist in any structural changes necessary to facilitate this programme of social responsibility. It is quite obvious why he was selected to be a part of this process for if his fingers are in the pie he cannot escape responsibility for the outcome.

Winston Morgan as one who was brought up in the Inner City was a valuable member of the Team. Winston and his wife, Beverly, are blessed with four children, two boys and two girls. He serves as the Financial Accountant to the Church at headquarters and one often observes his analytical approach in the discussions as one would expect him to do his books. I was not to escape his strict scrutiny when the time came round to my ministerial competence evaluation.

The late *Vernon Nelson* was an ordained Minister and pastor of one our largest churches situated at Lambert Road, Brixton, London. He had been involved in some aspects of social responsibility but was perceived by some of his colleagues as being too much concerned with social programmes. However, it was felt that his experience would greatly benefit the Site Team in its search for answers to the pressing questions of social concern. Vernon only attended one meeting, not because he was uninterested in the work of the Team, but at that time he was too busy with a project in his local church. He was also involved in developing better Police relationship with the Black community following the riots in Brixton in 1985. Monthly meetings were being held at his church between the Police, Clergy and other leaders of the Lambeth area working for better understanding. However, Vernon kept abreast of our work and was always ready to lend advice whenever requested to do so. He was married to Eva and they have five adult children and a few grand children. He and his wife had ministered in Jamaica for many years before joining the ministry in England. The late Vernon Nelson saw the completion of the project before his sudden death while on holiday in Florida, USA., in February 1989.

The only single male on the Site Team was *Arnold Kirlew* who joined as a replacement to Andrew Moore. Arnold was a consultant to the now famous Brent Community Project which was started by some young Blacks from one of the Independent Churches in London. I met Arnold at one of our church services in London, and after learning of his work at the Brent project I invited him to Overstone with a view to gleaning from his work and to see how our own social responsibility project could be pushed forward. Arnold was very enthusiastic to learn that at last the Church was willing to listen to the voice of the new generation. He was so full of ideas that I did not hesitate to ask him to get on board and he gladly responded. As it turned out, his contribution was most valuable.

(d) SITE TEAM EXPLORATION

The first meeting of the Site Team was held on 7 November 1985. After a time of sharing the Aims and Objectives of the project, each member was asked to present a short paper on mission and ministry to highlight these thoughts:

(a) my picture of the ideal Church

(b) what the Church is like now.

This formed the starting point of our search for the roots that would lead to a proper interpretation of the eschatological hope of the NTCG and to a better future for its people.

While the NTCG seeks to express the gospel in terms that could be understood and appreciated by its younger generation, it must not permit the theological hope of a literal return of Christ to be obliterated or obscured as some have done. Until he comes, this gospel must be preached not only to liberate men from their social evils as well as their personal sins; but must also direct them in the way in which it could be contextualized in their everyday living. Just as millions are lamenting the conditions which they describe as hell on earth; so we could rejoice in the fact that there can be a little bit of heaven down here.

The Site Team sensed the Biblical urgency for the NTCG to take a careful look at its social responsibility as we considered the account of the feeding of the five thousand as recorded in the Gospel of Mark 6.32-44. It is interesting that this is one of the few miracles of Christ that are recorded in both the Synoptics gospels and John. The disciples were caught up in the euphoria of the miracles they had just experienced in their ministry, and the teachings concerning the Kingdom of God. After Christ had ministered all day, it was now evening and the disciples told him to send the people away to go and find food. 'Send them away that they may go into the country round about, and lodge, and get victuals: for we are here in a desert place' (Luke 9.12). But Jesus sensing the urgency, said to them, 'Give you them to eat. To this the disciples replied that they could not afford it. If even they had two hundred penny loaves of bread, that could not suffice to feed the mass of people (Mark 6.37). Jesus then ordered them to bring what they had, and he blessed it, and gave it to them to feed the people. It was a little boy's lunch of five loaves and two fish that was used to feed over five thousand men, women and children. Here Jesus demonstrated to the disciples that, not only were the people to be fed the Word of God, but their bodily requirements were just as important in the Kingdom of God. How often this passage has been spiritualized to suggest that we must break the Word to the masses. But this is not the point, for the Word was already properly given. It was the physical need that was left unmet, and Christ demanded that that need be met.

The Site Team was careful to note the deception embodied in some popular views for liberation of the poor and oppressed. For instance, Andre Bieler and others see the Church's function as 'perpetually to present to the world the goals of peace, non-violence, liberty, solidarity, disarmament, classless society, global society etc., and to work for their political realization.'[1] But the Team felt that the

---

[1] Andre Bieler, *Politics of Hope*, trans. Dennis Pardee (Wm. B. Eerdmans, Grand Rapids, 1974), p.118.

NTCG could not support such a view. The stand taken by Robert Bellah was more in keeping with the direction they would want the Church to go. Bellah observes,

'Religion and morality and politics are not the same things and confusing them can lead to terrible distortions. But cutting all links between them can lead to even worse distortions.'[1]

The NTCG, having severed itself from the policy-making bodies of this country, had failed to make any important contribution to its people's struggle for survival. Our ardent hope was that by this process, the Church would be encouraged to heed the caution of Carl Henry to those who interpret the demands of the gospel as a decision of faith alone. For Henry,

'the gospel of Christ contains more than assurance of divine forgiveness and a new life; it includes also the seed of human dignity and freedom. To obscure this essential fact is no less to imperil the human soul than to neglect personal evangelism'.[2]

For those of us who had come to faith in Christ under the older generation, all we understood was to depend on God by faith for our needs. When these were not met, it was seen as our lot in life, for heaven was the answer to all life's earthly woes. Somehow, the fact that one should participate in the process of changing the evils of our society was alien to the faith; one's lot was beyond any hope of change in this instance.

What the Team would search for were the roots in Scripture that had been lost amidst the over-emphasized eschatological hope of the Church. The Scriptures are filled with examples of God's concern for the poor and oppressed, the widow and the fatherless. That Christ came to set physical captives free from hunger, poverty, squalor and neglect is the truth that the NTCG must aggressively pursue.

(c) PROBLEM STATEMENT

With such a history and background, it would seem obvious to the outsider that the NTCG had at some point overlooked some aspect of social responsibility. This, however, was not easily detected. The early meetings of the Site team were spent in searching for the causes of the declining growth and spirituality of the Church over the previous ten years. It took some serious reasoning and facing up to the issues before we could come to grips with the fact that the problem was our neglect of ministry to the whole person, and not just the spiritual. *There had been such an emphasis on preparing people for heaven that we had neglected to prepare them to live and participate in our present-day British society, and assist in any meaningful change.* The Team came to the conclusion that NTCG was to preach the message of redemption, and not forget its implications in every area of man's existence.

---

[1] Robert Bellah. 'American Civil Religion in 1970s' in *Anglican Theological Review*, July 1973 (Supplementary Series).
[2] *Christianity Today* Vol 19 No 20. 4 July 1975.

Having reached this point in our investigation, the necessary goals to improve the status of the Church had to be sought. The Site Team whose composition was detailed earlier in this chapter, agreed that two main goals should be attempted:

1. To increase the involvement of the NTCG in responding to the social and economic situation. This was to be facilitated by the setting up of the Department of Social Responsibility to assist the local Churches' understanding for the realization of such responsibilities. A systemic change in the national structure of the Church was necessary as the problem was seen to affect the entire organizational concept of ministry.

2. To sensitize the African Caribbean people to the benefits of cooperative endeavour.

The latter goal should be accomplished through a programme of Biblical and theological analysis, coupled with a project of setting up a cooperative venture in a needy area. It was felt that one of the main drawbacks among Blacks was their lack of co-operation in the struggle for survival. Some saw this fragmentation as resulting from the former Colonial theology which lent itself to individual choice, rather than corporate activity. The strategies involved in the achievement of these goals would be seen in the actual setting up of the various projects. The NTCG is expected to propagate a truth that not only takes men to heaven, but one that gives all of life's meaning in the present time, moment by moment. First, we must confess that we are persons made in the image of God, then members of the Church. The balance must be kept between its preaching and its practice. It must maintain strength in its beliefs that would produce the corresponding beauty in its communities. James rightly admonishes the Church:

'Suppose there are brothers or sisters who need clothes and don't have enough to eat. What good is there in your saying to them, God bless you! Keep warm and eat well, if you don't give them the necessities of life?' (James 2.15,16).

Our faith must be demonstrated in the here and now.

3. Facing the Issues

The NTCG in Great Britain has a firm commitment to a hope based on a theology yet to be realized, when Christ who will return, will reward each one according to one's faithfulness (Matthew 16.27). The faithful, therefore, were to be content with their lot in this life as a brighter day will dawn 'tomorrow'. With such protracted emphasis in preparing people for the promised heavenly mansions, there was little or no regard given for preparing them to live in this present British society, and to participate in bringing about any meaningful change. There is, therefore, an urgent necessity for the Church to face up to the issues of ministering to the whole person; not just to the spiritual, but to the material and temporal needs of its constituents.

Over the years, the financial and material resources of the Church were exhausted in promoting the numerical and spiritual growth of the Church. The Church grew rapidly, but in recent times the growth has slowed considerably. This was attributed largely to the unresponsive, permissive and secularized generation of the Seventies and early Eighties. The Site Team, however, recognizing the drift of the youth from the Church, and the hopelessness of the older members who often seem to be unaware of the happenings around them, perceive the problems as due to lack of the Church's involvement with the social issues of the day, and the effect this has had on its growth. This fact was clearly stated in interviews held with many of the youths of the Church and with some who had left the Church. In one such interview Arnold Kirlew, a Site Team member who represented the younger generation of the Church, identified three areas of deep concern in the Church as:

a. Unemployment
b. Breakdown of family unity
c. Youth's disregard for Church teachings

The general feeling was that the Church was inept it its attitude to social issues and failed to set Biblical and theological guidelines for its members. The platitudes and remonstration of a Sunday morning lecture did not, in some cases, deal with the issues that plagued the minds of the members during the week.

To some, it seemed the organization had been slow to come to grips with the plight of the elderly, many of whom came to Britain in the Fifties, and were now facing retirement but could not return to the Caribbean having spent the better part of their lives in this country. The middle-aged too, were constantly being laid off as factories closed and their jobs became redundant. The rising unemployment further dampened the hopes of the youth, many of whom have seen their fathers out of work for years, and their mothers as the only breadwinner for the family. Many of these now disadvantaged, disorganized, and disorientated people are unable to cope with the bleak and brutal winds of racism and prejudice in the limited job-market. Lacking in skills in specialized areas, they are losing the struggle for survival. Like the children of Israel in the time of the Judges when 'everyone did what was right in one's own eyes', some adult and aged people have lost hope, while some youths seek to 'drink at fountains that hold no water.' Many experiment with drugs and other vices that land them behind prison bars. A recent report showed that 45% of youths in prison were Black. The sad fact was that while all this was happening, the Church was still pursuing its traditional method of evangelizing and propagating its gospel. Little time was given to any scientific analysis of its failure to make new inroads, or create any meaningful impact on its younger generation.

(a) UNEMPLOYMENT

It is estimated that over 30% of some Church male members have been unemployed for the past 10 years. In some areas less than 50% have permanent jobs. Since the Church's base income is through tithes (one tenth of one's income) and offerings, the unemployment situation inevitably undermines the basic support system of the Church and ultimately its ability to execute its Biblical mandate.

Another fact that has to be borne out by surveys is that Black people usually have low-paid jobs and as a result earn less than the working population as a whole. They live mainly in the Inner Cities such as London, Birmingham, Leicester, Manchester, Bristol, Coventry and Bradford. Because of the great decline in industrial manual and semi-skilled and unskilled employment, Black unemployment has risen proportionately higher than the rest of the population. The following is an example of the trends.[1]

Table 1. Unemployment rate: Great Britain

	Autumn 1977 (England Only)	May 1977	1977	May 1973
Black People	9.2	7.9	7.7	5.3
All Unemployed	5.2	5.3	5.5	3.6

When these figures are compared with those of 1989 published by the Employment Gazette one finds that unemployment had risen higher among the non-Whites than for the Whites of similar circumstances. The rate for West Indian (African Caribbean) males was 15% as compared to White males at 6.9% as seen in Table 2.

Table 2. 1989 Unemployment rates by ethnic origin in Great Britain

	White	West Indian	Indian	Pakistani/ Bangla- deshi	All Ethnic
Male	6.9	15	10	18	8
Female	6.8	14	9	—	8

[1] *Department of Employment Gazette.*

Table 3. Unemployment rates for persons aged 16 and over in selected regions and metropolitan counties, by ethnic origin 1987-1989

Region of Residence	White	Ethnic minority Groups
England	9	14
North	13	2
Yorkshire & Humberside	10	17
East Midlands	8	15
East Anglia	6	*
South East	6	12
Greater London	7	13
Rest of South East	5	*
South West	7	*
West Midlands	9	22
North West	11	16
Wales	11	*
Scotland	12	*
Great Britain	?	?

* Estimates not shown

The Tables taken from the *Employment Gazette* of February 1991 is an attempt to portray the picture of Black or ethnic minority unemployment trends in Great Britain. I should venture to say that since 1977 the figures have not improved. While factors of qualification and age would have some effect on the unemployment rate in general, the analysis shows that '70% of ethnic minority, (80% of African Caribbean) lived in metropolitan county areas as compared with 30% White groups.' It went on to observe that:

'Ethnic minority group unemployment rates also vary according to region . . . Unemployment rates for the minority group population of working age in the years 1987-1989 were generally higher than the White population, and reflected the overall regional pattern of unemployment.'[1]

Over the years there are those who have divorced the work of evangelism from monetary concerns. The mentality of the Church has been that God will finance his programme of evangelism irrespective of the material position of the membership. Believers are constantly reminded that the Bible says, '. . . For every beast of the forest is mine, and the cattle upon a thousand hills' (Psalm 50.10). The inference is that material wealth is of little importance to God for he owns everything.

The younger generation of the Church are now more radical in their approach to money matters. While wishing to confirm the ability of God to provide their needs, some are more conscious of the necessity for personal involvement and initiative in achieving their own ambitions. The tension has developed when some have seen that there has been no response to their prayers and the Church is failing to provide a medium to assist them in terms of employment, money, self-confidence and trust. They feel God is not hearing them; the Church is not

---

[1] 'Unemployment and Ethnic Origin': Special feature in *Employment Gazette*, February 1991, pp.68, 70.

on their side; so they seek another road. Even some who are privileged to participate in some projects or schemes do so with much scepticism. They do not believe that the Government is genuinely concerned in providing employment, but that the Youth Training Schemes are a farce, or offer very little meaningful hope for the future. Coupled to that is the drastic cut-off of funding by some Borough Councils thus leaving the Luncheon Clubs and Day Centres destitute of funds to help the aged and needy.

(b) BREAKDOWN OF FAMILY UNITY

In former times the whole family went to Church, but today as some youngsters reach eighteen they seek their own accommodation and move away from home. This has not only created problems for them as many are unprepared to cope with the harsh economic and social pressures outside the home, but it has also placed a burden of the upkeep of the house on their parents who could have been assisted if the working children were with them. In the Caribbean, parents were used to the support of working children living at home (a cultural survival of the African extended family system). The young British children of African Caribbean descent, however, are more acculturated to the British system and as such, leave their parents to paddle their own canoe.

There is also the problem of homelessness that is sweeping the country. This is compounded by the fact that youngsters leave home and flock to the cities in search of work, and more often, just to get away from what they perceive to be too much parental control. A recent report claimed that over two million young people between the ages of 16 to 19 are homeless, and 150 thousand are added to the list each year. In London alone, over three thousand are sleeping roughly on the streets, under bridges, and abandoned buildings. Of greater concern is the fact that Black people are over represented in these figures to the tune of 40%. Such conditions tend to lead youngsters into drugs and prostitution.

For some Black youths the Church is the only family they have. It is expected that an environment would be provided that would care for their personal concerns and become the family support mechanism. When this cannot be found, the youngsters seek it in other undesirable avenues. It is not sufficient for the Church to provide them a sedative 'to put them under,' or give them a 'high' on Sunday when they have to face the problems and insecurities on Monday without the assurance that the organization is with them in their struggles.

The break-down of family unity also led to premature marriages. Lacking parental guidance on matters of sexuality and family responsibilities, many of such marriages have failed with resulting emotional and financial problems landed on the family. There has also been an alarming increase of single-parent families due to the changing moral values of society. These single-parent families are often left to the mercies of the Social Services, with little support from the Church which often views their circumstances with much displeasure.

(c) YOUTH'S REGARD FOR CHURCH TEACHINGS

To the older generation, the teachings of the Church are sacrosanct. They unquestioningly follow the doctrines and teachings of the NTCG. The youths on the other hand, are of the opinion that the Church has not kept pace with the modern, scientific, economic and political arguments as they relate to issues of life. While some openly reject the teachings as archaic, traditional and even mere Caribbean cultural taboos, there are others who earnestly seek guidance on matters of faith and practice.

One of such issues that has greatly affected the church and is potentially very divisive is the matter of Christian adornment. Like most Holiness Movements of the late 1800s, Church of God members were expected to live a life free from sinful practices, and to shun pleasures and activities that would seem to be inconsistent with holy living. One of these was the way Christians adorn themselves.

In the formative days when the Church ruled on members' ethical behaviour, it was held 'That the wearing of unnecessary jewelry for ornament or decoration be made a test of membership in the Church, in conformity with the teachings of the Bible' (Isaiah 52.2; 1 Peter 3.3). This was done at the 25th General Assembly, 1930. This became accepted practice in all the churches in the U.S.A. and other areas of the world where the Church existed. In some cases, even wedding bands were not permitted, and today, among the older folks, some still refuse to wear the wedding band.

In 1936, at the 31st General Assembly, it was passed that wearing of rings, bracelets, and earrings for mere outward show was sinful and so prohibited. This further endorsed the earlier teaching of the Church. The statement in the Minutes of the 31st General Assembly read:

> 'Against members wearing jewelry for ornament or decoration, such as finger rings (this does not apply to wedding bands), bracelets, earrings lockets etc. (1 Timothy 2.9; 1 Peter 3.3)'.[1]

Generally, most members conformed to this teaching but, as the Church grew world-wide, it soon became evident that this would pose a problem for those in other cultures who did not perceive this custom of adornment as sinful, but rather, as a part of their cultural dress. In time there was a gradual eroding of the teaching until the issue was brought to the Assembly for study and debate. The pressure for change increased in the Eighties as many saw that such restrictive teachings did not conform to the modern concepts of holiness; nor could the Scripture texts used to support them stand up to proper biblical exegesis. The younger generation argued that holiness had nothing to do with what went on the outside; holiness was to do with the heart. Therefore, one should not be judged by outward appearance.

After much heated and prolonged debate, at the 63rd General Assembly held at Forth Worth, Texas, in 1988, the following measure pertaining to adornment was approved:

Modest Appearance
We will demonstrate the scriptural principle of modesty by appearing and dressing in a manner that will enhance our Christian testimony and will avoid pride, elaborateness or sensuality.

---

[1] Supplement to Minutes of 59th General Assembly of the Church of God, p.7.

A. Modesty

According to the biblical idea, modesty is an inner spiritual grace that recoils from anything unseemly and impure, is chaste in thought and conduct, and is free from crudeness and indecency in dress and behaviour (Ephesians 4.25, 29, 31; 5. 1-8; 1 Timothy 2.9, 10). Therefore, modesty includes our appearance, dress, speech, and conduct and can be applied to all situations. The essential issue is, does our style of life please or displease God?

B. Appearance and Dress

Our life, character, and self-image are reflected by our apparel and mode of dress. The admonition of Scripture, 'Be not conformed to this world,' reminds us that our manner of dress must be modest and decent (Romans 12.2; 1 Thessalonians 5.22, 23). It is not displeasing to God for us to dress well and be well groomed. However, above all we must seek spiritual beauty which does not come from outward adornment with jewelry, expensive clothes or cosmetics, but good works, chaste conversation, and a meek and quiet spirit (Philipians 4.8; 1 Peter 3.3-5).

C. Pride, Elaborateness, Sensuality

As godly people we are to abstain from all lusts of the flesh and avoid dressing in a manner that encourages immoral thoughts, attitudes, and lifestyles (Galatians 5.13-21; 1 Peter 2.11; 2 Peter 1.4). Our beauty does not depend on elaborate, showy dress; extravagant, costly attire; or on the use of jewelry or cosmetics, but on our relationship with Christ. External adornment, whether clothing or jewelry, as an outward display of personal worth, is contrary to a spiritual attitude (James 2.1-4).'[1]

After this measure was passed, some members (young and old), saw it as a removal of the former inhibitions and it was left to one's conscience to decide whether to wear or not to wear jewelry. To others, since the Bible had not changed, and since the 25th General Assembly held that the practice was contrary to the Bible; the practice was still wrong. Those who felt strongly about it concluded that to start putting on the things which they took off years ago was yielding to the pressure of worldliness that had gripped society with the growth of the cosmetic and fashion industry. It would seem that this issue called for someone as wise as Solomon to decide whose child the practice belonged to. Either the child is on God's side or of the world.

As far as the writer is concerned, the overriding factor is 'Am I by my actions bringing glory to God or self?' Is it something that I would consider giving up if it would help to maintain the unity within the body of believers? It might well be this is one of those issues that the Apostle Paul would apply his principle:

'All things are lawful for me, but all things are not helpful. All things are lawful for me, but I will not be bought under the power of any.' (1 Corinthians 6.12, New King James Bible)

---

[1] Minutes, 63rd General Assembly of Church of God, pp. 108, 109.

The call to believers to live holy lives, especially in these last days when moral values are changing so rapidly, is not a call to live sanctimoniously, but a call for separation from worldliness which so glaringly displays itself in our Churches today. The natural man will most certainly find such stipulations objectionable, but those who would have their consciences informed by the Word of God, would not find it difficult to forego such practices for the sake of Christ. After all Christ has suffered for us, is it too much to suffer for him out of concern for others?

Another area of concern is the growth in the secular community-based organizations which has attracted many of the young people away from what they perceived as the narrow confines of the Church. Political awareness (the fact that the Church is apolitical) forced some to leave and align themselves with political parties. They have felt that the Parties can help them to understand life's meaning in the here and now, and thus they contribute their time and money to them. These same young people once gave that time and support to the Church, but now seek recognition on political platforms.

The Church too, has always been the seed-bed for the growth and development of the rich musical talents of Blacks. But, to a large extent, many Black youths have not found the Church capable of providing the extended platform for their talents when full grown. They, therefore, seek opportunity at secular studios to fulfil their careers. And too, in the mind of some members, the more educated and enlightened members seek fulfilment outside the Church. It naturally follows that it is made poorer, not only in financial terms, but in human resources. This tragic loss of potential leadership deprive the younger ones of role models, and is felt in many areas of the organization. The condition could have been different, had the organization guided its members in dealing with the secular world in the light of its teachings and its practical commitments. Serious consideration has now to be made, as there are others on the verge of joining the band-wagon of opportunists in search of their own fortunes.

Youths of the Nineties share deep concern regarding the Church's teaching with regard to a Christian's social life in what is acceptable and permissible behaviour. There appears to be a serious problem stemming from the cultural gap' between the members born in the Caribbean and those born in Britain. Years ago, the older members carried with them from the Caribbean the belief that Christians' indulgence in sports, such as cricket, football, swimming etc. was robbing the time and energy that should be spent in more spiritual activities. Often they would quote the Apostle Paul as saying, '... bodily exercise profits little' (1 Timothy 4. 8). One pastor's son regrettably informed me that he felt his pastor was insensitive to his ambitions and aspirations in the area of sports. He had requested permission from his pastor to run on a Sunday as he was selected to represent the whole of London in a sporting event (he was a sporting peer of the now famous Linford Christie). The response from his pastor was a stern rebuke, reminding him that there were other days to run besides Sunday which was a day of worship. The young man took his own decision and left the Church.

Today, he is a successful coach, but is aggrieved that he had to leave because of his pastor's interpretation of acceptable behaviour, and not because he had lost faith in God.

The Church also taught against 'mixed bathing with the opposite sex,' and up until 1988, this was a test of membership. This teaching was impractical to comply with in the eyes of some members. It seemed impossible for one to go to the swimming pool, or to the beaches without having to mix with others of the opposite sex. Some also felt that the teaching was tantamount to a prohibition against swimming altogether, or expecting one to be rich enough to afford a swimming pool in one's own back-yard. Members of school age where swimming was a normal curicular activity, found this prohibition most impossible and unreasonable.

Of even greater concern is the matter of continence and marital fidelity. The Church has always stood against sexual relations outside of marriage. With the changing values of this modern society, many unmarried members face pressures to conform to the times. For, to one who has not been informed in the Judeo-Christian ethics which acknowledges that the believer is to live under the supernatural order of redemption, the Church's insistence that pre-marital or extra-marital sexual behaviour leads to moral turpitude is considered to be traditional, Victorian, and unacceptable in today's society.

Some of these issues were raised at a meeting I had with pastors' children between the ages of fifteen and twenty-five, in an effort to identify their areas of concern. There is a high rate of backsliding among pastors' children. For most of them, their problems stemmed from a question of identity. They felt under pressure by Church members to conform to certain patterns of behaviour and, act as pastors children' even though no one took time to explain what that particular behaviour pattern was supposed to be. Some, as a result, became resentful, detached, snobbish or even gave up the struggle to conform. Some complied so as to prevent their parents being dismissed from the pastorate. They were told that Paul questioned, '. . . if a man know not how to rule his own house, how shall he take care of the Church of God?' (1 Timothy 3. 5). One pastor's son remarked, 'We feel pressurized into becoming pattern setters, or to keep up with our parent's image. Often we suffer from a personality conflict, i.e., what we know we are or would like to be versus what others expect us to be, or want us to become.'

One encouraging fact was that among the group were some pastors' children who enjoyed their role and found it a privilege to be part of their parents' ministry. Some also had a desire to become pastors themselves. However, these were in the minority.

Given that the issues of unemployment, breakdown of family unity, and the youth's regard for Church teachings are pressing issues that will have decisive effects on the Church and its community, the demand for positive action by the Church leaders can no longer be ignored. The Church must be concerned about social justice and material needs of its community as well as the righteousness of the Kingdom. The admonition of Dietrich Bonhoeffer is quite applicable to this situation for he notes:

> 'To give bread to the hungry man is not the same as to proclaim the grace of God and justification to him, and to have received bread is not the same as to have faith. Yet for him who does these things for the sake of the ultimate, and in the knowledge of the ultimate, this penultimate does bear a relation - to the ultimate.'[1]

To ignore the penultimate while striving to achieve the ultimate is a denial of present realities. This is the naked fact the NTCG must face.

4. In Search of a Better Life

Learie Constantine, born in Diego Martin, near Port of Spain, Trinidad, in 1901, came to England on a cricket tour with his West Indian team in 1923. Returning with his team in 1928, he distinguished himself by outstanding performances on the field, scoring 1000 runs and taking 100 wickets. He and his wife, Norma, then decided to settle in Nelson, Lancashire, where he took a job playing in Lancashire League. He, however, continued to play for the West Indies until 1939.

When the Second World War broke out, Learie was employed as a welfare officer by the Ministry of Labour to look after the interest of West Indians working in Manchester. After the war, he studied Law and became a barrister and spent his new-found knowledge to fight for the civil rights of Blacks. He unrelentingly exposed discrimination and even won a court case against a well-known hotel that refused him room because he was Black.

Returning to Trinidad in 1958, he won election to Parliament, and was made Minister of Works, but later returned to England as High Commissioner for Trinidad and Tobago. In 1962 he was knighted. After resigning his post as Commissioner, he returned to his legal career and became a member of the Race Relations Board. He received local and national fame and was given freedom of the Borough of Nelson in 1963. He served as a governor of the BBC and received his life peerage in 1969. Before his death on 1 July 1971, Lord Constantine had found a better life.

Recently, I met and interviewed a member of our church at Harrow, Elaine Jackson, who hails from St. Anns Bay, Jamaica. She came to England in 1948 and attended Barnet Technical College where she gained seven GCE O' level passes. Elaine then began nursing training at the Barnet General Hospital where she qualified, gaining her SRN (now RGN). She pursued a Midwifery course at Barnet, and completed it at Bushey Heath, Hertfordshire, in 1956. After completion she worked as Staff Midwife, and later as a Sister at Harrow General from 1960-1965. Elaine became a Health Visitor in 1969, and in 1972 she was seconded to Hammersmith College of Further Education to set up a Family Liaison Scheme for counselling African Caribbean students entering further education. In those days, many students seeking further education in Britain found difficulty with the Grant procedure. Some could not cope with the new culture and this led to a breakdown in relationships with their parents. Elaine was to be a catalyst between students and parents. This pilot scheme conducted by the Hammersmith Community Relations Council was successful and was later funded by the Inner London Education Authority (ILEA).

Elaine pursued further Diploma and degree courses in middle management and nursing. However, she ended her career as a Nursing Tutor at the Royal Free Hospital where she took early retirement and opened her own Nursing Home.

Her social involvement included work as a member of the Association of Jamaicans since 1970; Education officer in 1974; and delegate from the West

Indian Standing Conference to United Nations Women's Committee between 1974-1976. She served as Chairman of the Community Relations Council for Harrow (now Council for Racial Equality), a position she held for twelve years. In 1982 she was recommended to serve as a Magistrate and began her work on the bench in 1984. Elaine feels she found a better life.

The story of Lord Constantine and Mrs Elaine Jackson have been highlighted as examples of those who came and found a better life in Britain. But this has not been the case of the large majority. For them, Britain has been a disappointment, a nightmare, a trap from which there is no escape. The majority of ethnic and Black people in particular believe that the system is discriminatory, and loaded with racism. It is difficult to convince the average Black person that there is any hope for the future in Britain. Such is the sorry state of affairs of this growing restless and disadvantaged people who came in search of a better life.

It must not be assumed that this hopelessness is peculiar to Blacks and ethnics alone; the frustration is no less common among some of the indigenous White population who tend to see the falling economy and rising unemployment as the result of the Blacks and Asians in their country. It is ironic that the indigenous people blame their plight on the immigrants in their land, while the immigrants or 'settlers' see their socio-economic problems as the result of the policies and exploitation of their lands by former British governments who owned them. Blacks and Ethnics bemoan the fact that their countries' wealth, both natural and human, were wantonly exploited and used to build up this country which seems to make no room for them. The situation is further exacerbated by rising unemployment, escalating crime and violence in the nation.

On reflection, one may ask the question, how did these sociological, economic and political factors combine to place African Caribbeans in this situation? A brief review at this stage might suffice:

1. THE 'COMMONWEALTH IDEAL'

The settlement of 'immigrants' in the United Kingdom Colonies in the 1950s and their expectations were encouraged by:
—military service—large numbers of West Indian personnel fought with others for Britain in both World Wars.
—commerce—banking and the processing of 'Third World' products led to Imperial (or Commonwealth) preference as an adopted policy.
  'The time came when this loosely knit world-spread association . . . was confronted with the most searching test of all. The Mother Country . . . this famous Island . . . seemed to enter the very jaws of death . . . Then, surely, was the moment for the Empire to break up . . . But in that dark terrific and also glorious hour, we received from all parts of HM Dominions, from the smallest to the greatest . . . the assurance that we would all go down or come through together' (Winston Churchill, in a speech in 1943).[1]

---

[1] Nigel & Power, *Black Settlers in Britain* p.82.

Most of the early settlers in Britain came here as British citizens and were proud of their status. However, the 1960s saw a dramatic change when many of the West Indian countries were given independence largely by Conservatives; ironically, the party of Empire. Britain, bereft of her overseas possessions, became one among other members of the Commonwealth. This led to former British citizens living in the country to be regarded as 'settlers' or 'immigrants'.

2. RACISM

Racism as an ideological concept is perceived as making genetically determined characteristics of a person the determining factor of that person's place in society, and his/her personal ability. Racism has been used politically and economically to justify domination, inequality and discrimination against one group of people to the detriment of the other. During the last World War, Black and White people fought side by side against Hitler's racism. The end of the war, however, saw a devaluation in the regard for Black people, and a return to the racist ideologies of earlier centuries

Unfortunately, racism is sometimes transmitted through education, i.e., school text books, songs etc. Attitudes and inflammatory remarks against Blacks are absorbed by children even at a tender age. My own son at the age of four was attending a kindergarten where he was the only Black. One day he came home and asked his mother, 'Mum, why did God make me black?' His Mum soon learnt that his peer, a little girl, had told him that 'Blacks are dirty.' Evidently this little girl had heard the remark from some adult and was unable to assess its true implications and the effect it would have on my son, and hence she repeated it.

Racism is also institutionalized in structures of society, in Housing and Employment. Parliament has acknowledged this fact and introduced legislation to deal with it. The 1976 Act made it unlawful to discriminate on basis of 'race', either directly or indirectly, in areas of Employment—(Section 4), Education—(Section 17), the provision of Goods and Services—(Section 20), Advertising—(Section 29). 'Incitement to racial hatred' was also made a criminal offence—(Section 70). Local Authorities were left with the duty to 'eliminate unlawful discrimination and to promote equality of opportunity and good race relations between different racial groups'.[1]   The Commission for Racial Equality was set up by this 1976 Race Relations Act, with duties:

 (i) working towards the elimination of discrimination;
 (ii) promoting equality of opportunity and good race relations between per-
      sons of different racial groups generally; and
(iii) keeping under review the working of the Act. 4

In the 1991 Annual Report of the Commission for Racial Equality to the Rt. Hon. Kenneth Baker MP, Secretary of State for the Home Department, Mr.

---

[1] For further reading on plight of Blacks, see David Smith, *The Facts of Racial Disadvantage* (Penguin, London, 1977); F. Klung and P. Gordon, *Different Worlds: Racism and Discrimination in Britain*, (Runnymede Trust, London, 1983).

Michael Day, Chairman of the Commission; is reported to have said:
'It may be impossible to establish whether there is more or less racism and discrimination now than 25 years ago. Direct discrimination is generally covert, and indirect discrimination a product of ordinary practices not often recognized as being unlawful by those who operate them.'
He went on to warn that
'many of the social factors which contributed to the inner city disturbances of ten years ago are still apparent: high levels of unemployment, poor housing, health, education and welfare facilities.'
It seemed clear to him that there was an increasing sense of disillusionment and despair' among Blacks.[1]

Racism is alleged to be practised in the Criminal Justice System and experienced by Black people as they search for a better life. Many are made criminals simply because they happen to be at the wrong place at the wrong time. It is alarming that in a society where the Black population is only 5%, a large proportion of people appearing in courts, and that are inmates of the prisons, are Black. Some are there, not because they have criminal intentions; but rather, as simple rural folk coming into this sophisticated society searching for personal betterment, they were ignorant of the laws and mores of the land. The 1982 report of the Director of Prisons Department included the following information:
—In the young offender institutions at Rochester, Blantyre and Dover, the Black population was 30%
—In three dispersal prisons in the South-East, the Black population was 15%.[2]

Another report by the Policy Studies Institute indicated that Black people' in general are more likely to be stopped by Police than White people. For instance, young Black males in London have nearly a 50% chance of being stopped along the street, compared to a 16% chance for other Londoners. Similarly, young Black males driving cars can expect to be stopped five times in the course of a year. Yet the proportion of stops which leads to a detection of an offence is about one in twelve. There is evidence which also highlights the fact that Black people are less likely to get protection from the Police. According to *New Humanity*, a Home Office study (1981) on racist violence against Ethnic people, Asian people are 50 times more likely, and African Caribbean people 36 times more likely to experience racist attacks than White people.[3]

It will be obvious from the foregoing that the chances of the average person of African Caribbean descent finding a better life on the social, political and economic levels in this country are very bleak; and in particular, the prospects of the British-born Blacks even more elusive, if these conditions remain unchanged.

---

[1] CRE Central Office, Elliot House, London.
[2] Reported in the *Voice*, 18 June 1991.
[3] Conlan & Hobbs, *New Humanity*, Unit 9.

3. RACE AND IMMIGRATION

In preparation for the General Election held in June 1987, the four main political parties published in their manifestos their plans for dealing with the question of Race and Immigration. These were as follows:

(1) Labour Party

The Party's policies on employment, education, housing, health care and local government would be of equal benefit to the 'whole community' including Black people. A Labour government would 'take firm action to promote racial equality, attack racial discrimination, and encourage contract compliance and other positive means of ensuring equity for all citizens.'

The manifesto also promised that Labour would take firm action against racial attacks. On immigration, Labour would be firm and fair and ensure that the Law does not discriminate against race, colour or sex.

(2) SDP/Liberal Alliance

An Alliance government promised to enact the European Convention into British Law to enable citizens to have redress in British courts.

On Immigration, the Alliance planned to 'repeal the sexist and racist aspects of the British Nationality Act' 1981, and to seek to return to everyone born in Britain the right to citizenship.

On Housing and Employment, the Alliance was to take positive steps to secure equal opportunities for racial minorities.

But it was the Conservatives that won the day and their policies were:

On Immigration, to 'tighten the existing Law to ensure that control over settlement becomes even more effective'. The manifesto stated that visitors from Ghana, Nigeria and the Indian sub-continent would require visas. On the question of equality, the manifesto stated that 'reverse discrimination is itself injustice' and that equality cannot be obtained by such practices. The Conservative party was desirous of seeing all ethnic minorities participating fully in British culture . They will suffer permanent disadvantage if they remain in linguistic cultural ghettoes.[1]

Noting that violence lay deep in the society, the Conservative manifesto continued to state that Government would increase the power police can use and planned to increase the number of the police and strengthen the special constabulary.

The Conservative Government kept to its manifesto and brought the Immigration Bill before Parliament. Diane Abbot, the first Black woman member of Parliament described the bill as 'squalid, cruel and racist.'[2] The Labour Shadow Home Secretary, Roy Hattersley, described it as the most tawdry little Bill he had seen in his twenty-three year Parliamentary career', wrote Stephen Goodwin in *The Independent*. He went on to quote Mr Hattersley's rejection of the Bill as one whose 'purpose is for Government to continue polishing its image

---

[1] Race & Immigration, *Runnymede Trust* June 1987, No 204 p.1,2.
[2] *The Independent*, 17 November 1987.

as a party which is hard on Immigration. The families which are adversely affected by this Bill will inevitably be of Black and Asian origin, and almost invariably poor.'[1]

Not only was this Bill applied requiring people from Ghana, Nigeria and the Indian Sub-continent to obtain visas, but in recent times, visitors from the Caribbean and Jamaica in particular, have been heavily scrutinized at Immigration and many have been refused entry. In many cases this is perceived as racist action on the part of the officials.

Another election looms ahead at the time of writing, and in the next few months of the life of this Parliament, the Government would seek to further tighten immigration laws against asylum seekers in search of a better life.

There are also deep-seated fears that, when the barriers come down for the rest of Europe in 1992, other barriers will be raised against African Caribbeans with resident status in this country. At the time when persons of Caribbean nationality were allowed to register as British citizens—even though at a price—some did not take the opportunity for they were told there would be no difference between British passport holders and those nationals with only resident permits. Now, some of these persons complain of experiencing delays at immigration on returning to Britain from trips abroad. The fears, whether real or unfounded, are causing a measure of unrest. The sudden changes that have taken place in Eastern Europe and the re-unification of Germany makes the situation even more precarious; there are no Race Relation Laws in Common Market countries as exist in Britain. It is left to be seen how these Laws will be interpreted in the new Europe.

At a meeting sponsored by the British Council of Churches, at which I was a participant, the issue of racism in all areas of British Society was discussed. The conference called upon the Churches (Black and White) to unite their efforts to combat racism which was growing as a cancer in the society. Though destructive in its mildest forms, it was being overlooked and fostered in many unlikely places.

The NTCG must accept the challenge to respond to racism in the society, not only for its own survival, but because racism is alien to the principles of the gospel of Christ. It is for that reason that the Church wishes to be identified as a 'Church' not a 'Black Church' as though for Black people alone. The NTCG has a message for all people. If it is right for a White pastor to minister to Black people successfully, there should be no contradiction to a Black pastor ministering to White people, for God's Spirit is not limited to race. When Peter had learnt this rudimentary Biblical truth and was confronted with his racist past, he confessed:

'Most certainly and thoroughly I now perceive and understand that God shows no partiality and is no respecter of persons, but in every nation he who venerates and has a reverential fear of God, treating him with worshipful obedience and living uprightly, is acceptable to him and sure of being received and welcomed by him' (Acts 10.34, 35, Amplified Bible).

[1] *Ibid.*

The NTCG will seek to teach and strive for racial harmony and justice in the society and especially within the Church. Black and White people will have to live and work together; not as in the past, in a master/slave relationship, but as '... fellow-citizens ... of the household of God' (Eph. 2.19).

Without and within the NTCG are thousands of Blacks whose search for a better life has reached a dead end in terms of their material existence. Their hope for social mobility and economic stability has constantly been undermined purely because of the stereotyping in the wider society. If one were tuned into their wavelength, one could hear them say:

I Notice When all the eye contact is between White people excluding Black people

I Notice when White people address only each other

I Notice when a Black person speaks it falls on deaf ears

But later if a White person says the same things it is heard as important.

Or what a Black person said is attributed to Whites.

I Notice that Black people are more often interrupted by White people than the other way round.

That topics initiated by White people get more air time than the ones generated by Black people

When a Black person speaks, they represent their own point of view and these are discounted, for they speak for all Black people—not as an individual

> Yes, I Notice
> I Hear I See I Hurt
> and I Wonder!   (Unknown).

5. A More Excellent Way

Since its arrival in Britain, the NTCG has strongly emphasized a spiritual ministry. In seeking to propagate its particular kind of evangelicalism in a post-Christian British society, it neglected the socio-economic needs of its members, thus being unbalanced in its presentation of the ministry of Christ to the whole person. In addition, programmes were projected mainly to Church members and not to facilitate the wider community.

In spite of the fact that a few Churches had sought to engage in some social projects, it was not Church policy; and, as such, the head office never encouraged or suggested the development of any co-ordinated system of machinery which would enable its members to progress in technical and non- traditional areas of work. Consequently, the Church had not adequately stressed the issues of social mobilization, political awareness, economic development, and co-operative participation; and more significantly, the role that individual Christians were required to play without compromising their faith. This resulted in some of the more educated members perceiving the Church as being out of touch with reality and unable, or unwilling, to address itself to current issues that affect the everyday life of the community. The need was therefore urgent for the Church to seek to correct this perception by actively becoming an influential voice in addressing the issues that affect its growing number of young people, the ageing constituents, and marginalized, powerless Black people in general.

(a) BIBLICAL PRECEDENT

The question then arises, are there any Biblical examples that this strictly' Biblically centred Church failed to discover in its response to social issues? Is there a more excellent way to be found in the Holy Word that has not been explored to shed light, and give guidance to a people seeking to live between this age and the age to come?

To the modern youth, one of the arguments against our brand of Christianity is that a radical commitment to the person of Jesus Christ is incompatible with the modern problems of power and progress. To them it seems that all Jesus is about is loving one's enemies, having godly sorrow for sin, and keeping oneself free from moral turpitude. And that is to be the only pre-occupation of the Church. As far as they are concerned, when one is faced with the problem of social responsibility, one should go to sources other than the Bible. This is no surprise because the average Christian is rather unaware of the nature of social institutions and powers. They have not fully grasped the fact that power originated with God, and all that is needed is to discern the hand of God in the affairs of this world. The apostle Paul clearly stated in Colossians 1. 15—17:

'He is the image of the Invisible God, the firstborn of every creature. For in him were created all things, those in heaven and those on earth, visible and invisible; whether thrones or dominions or principalities or powers; all was created through him. And he is above all things, and all things subsist in him' (*New International Version*).

The word 'subsist' has the root meaning of system, i.e., in him all things are systematized. God is not divorced from the affairs of this world. A God who is concerned only with our spiritual relationship to him and is unconcerned how we fare in this world's systems will be denying his role of being Lord. No wonder Christ reminded us 'If you being evil know how to give good gifts unto your children, how much more shall your Father which is in heaven give good things to them that ask him?' (Matt. 7.11).

One of the strongest images that describe the realities of the Black experience is the Babylonian captivity of the children of Israel. In this, God's concern for the social well being of his trusting ones can be clearly seen. Although they were exiled in great humiliation because of their disobedience and idolatrous living, God instructed Jeremiah to send them a message of hope which created much controversy and suspicion in the eyes of his contemporaries, and was considered to be capricious and treasonous.

Nebuchadnezzar's armies had taken the people of God away captive to Babylon. The city was destroyed and laid waste. The prophets were predicting that speedy deliverance would come to the captives thus offering a false hope. But Jeremiah, directed by the Lord, wrote to the captives in Babylon:

'This is what the Lord Almighty, God of Israel, says to all those I carried into exile from Jerusalem to Babylon: "Build houses and settle down; plant gardens and eat what they produce. Marry and have sons and daughters; find wives for your sons and give your daughters in marriage; so that they too may have sons and daughters. Increase in number there; do not decrease. Also seek the peace and prosperity of the city to which I have carried you into exile. Pray to the Lord for it, because if it prospers, you too will prosper." Yes this is what the Lord Almighty the God of Israel says: "Do not let the prophets and diviners among you deceive you. Do not listen to the dreams you encourage them to have. They are prophesying lies to you in my name. I have not sent them", declares the Lord' (Jer. 29.4-9 (N.I.V)).

The captives were not to be disconcerted by despair; nor allow their diviners and prophets to deceive them, but they were to settle down and build the society, as it was still God's desire for them to enjoy the fruits of the riches of Babylon even while in exile.

Among those who were carried away captive into Babylon were Daniel, Hananiah, Mishael and Azariah, according to the Book of Daniel.[1]

However, if we take the book at its face value, those young men among others, obeyed Jeremiah's message and did not isolate themselves from the position of power that became open to them while they awaited the deliverance promised

---

[1] Many modern scholars do not accept that the Book of Daniel belongs to this period or was even written by Daniel. According to Freeman, its authenticity was first challenged by the Neoplatonist Porphyry, who claimed that the book was a forgery and was probably written during the Maccabean period, since the book, in his opinion, gave details of that period. Modern scholars place the date around 167 BC. Hobart E. Freeman, *An introduction to the Old Testament Prophets* (Moody Press, Chicago, 1968), p.251.

by God. They participated in the political, economic and social affairs of the Babylonian community, and rose to positions of great power and influence. It is recorded that Daniel became the chief of the three presidents who were set over the one hundred and twenty princes King Darius set to rule the whole kingdom. Daniel proudly maintained his faith in his God in the face of stiff opposition from his Babylonian counterparts. Even when a plot was made against his life, he did not compromise his faith, but was more resolute in his commitment to his God for which his faith was rewarded and his enemies defeated (Daniel 6. 1-24).

The three Hebrew boys, Shadrach, Meshach, and Abednego (the Babylonian names given to Hananiah, Mishael and Azariah), while rising to positions of influence and power in Nebuchadnezzar's government, refused to bow to his idols, and demonstrated that their God was able to deliver them from the flames of destruction (Dan. 3. 19-27).

All these Biblical examples show that it is possible for one to maintain an indomitable faith in God, and not live in isolation from the affairs and realities of the world. It is evidence for our youth that it is no sin to be involved socially, educationally and politically in the affairs of the British society as long as they maintain their faith in God. Too many have left the Church because they were made to feel that such activities were incompatible with their spiritual commitments, and were evidences of worldly ambitions. The NTCG leaders need to recognize that one can better serve the community and assist in building the Kingdom of God; not by separating the material from the spiritual, but by allowing the spiritual to impact upon the material. This knowledge will enable the Church to work to help redress the economic violence that has exercised a demonic influence over Blacks and their progress. This lack of understanding has deprived many of them of access to the basic goods necessary for subsistence. Some still live 'hand to mouth' after years of hard work in this country. Many have not realized their potential for they have never been given a chance, while others have not utilized the opportunities that they have been privileged to gain by being here. The Bible reveals that God is concerned about everyone's future, both here and hereafter. Believers are to literally 'occupy till he comes' (Luke 19.13); not indulging in idle speculative dreams that all things will be put right at the eschaton, but working assiduously to build a better community here and now.

(b) THEOLOGICAL CONSIDERATION

One of the conditions of being a member or minister of the NTCG is the affirmation of its credal profession according to the Minutes of the General Assembly. This requires the full acceptance of all the traditionally held theologies without critical reflection. To question the faith, in the mind of some, would indicate disloyalty to the Church. However, the tensions of this modern age demand an honest searching of the Scriptures to provide direction to those who seek a hope in the future. As Gustavo Gutierrez observed, 'theology is critical reflection on praxis in the light of the Word of God.'[1] If the NTCG is to be involved in a ministry of social responsibility, there is a necessity for examination of its chiliastic beliefs, for there are those who have taken on the struggle for social justice and perceive that alone as the realization of the Kingdom. This can have a debilitating effect on the evangelical mission of the Church.

Perhaps the way into the subject is to seek to understand the nature of the Kingdom of God. John the Baptist came preaching that the Kingdom of God was at hand (Matthew 3.2). Jesus Christ, after his baptism by John also preached that the Kingdom of God was at hand, but with a new dimension. He said, '... The Kingdom of God comes not by observation neither shall they say, Lo here! or lo there! for, behold, the Kingdom of God is within you' (Luke 17.20, 21). At other times, it would seem that he would refer to the Kingdom as some future event (Matthew 25.31, 34).

When the question is now put to the Church, the answers from the theologians vary according to their eschatological hope. Some of the views expressed are totally contradictory. For instance, some like Adolf von Harnack would see the Kingdom of God as the subjective realm of the spirit and its relationship to God. It is that power that enters and lays hold upon the human soul. C. H. Dodd on the other hand, sees the Kingdom of God as being experienced reality through the life of Jesus Christ. His coming brought the Kingdom of God from the 'sphere of speculative hope' to one of realized eschatology.'[2] In his opinion the death of Jesus Christ was not to usher in the Kingdom, for he had announced that the Kingdom of God had come.

For Dodd, the Kingdom of God is present when we can answer as Jesus did to John, 'the blind see, the lame walk, the lepers are cleansed, the deaf hear, the dead are raised, the poor have the gospel preached to them.' The healing ministry of Jesus was in his view, 'realized eschatology', that is to say, 'the impact upon this world of the "powers of the world to come" in a series of events unprecedented and unrepeatable, now in actual process.'[3]

For centuries the prophets had predicted that a deliverer would come who would be sovereign ruler of this evil world. Now that Jesus has come, the hope is realized. God has acted in human history. The strong man has been bound, and his kingdom spoiled. The Church then must rejoice in the victory that was wrought by Christ.[4] Dodd takes the position that the view of a Kingdom to come is part of the apocalyptic speculations of Jewish writers. He states:

> 'We have. it appears, no warrant in the teaching of Jesus for affirming that the long cycles of history will lead inevitably to a millennial "Kingdom Come" on earth. But we have warrant for affirming that God comes to meet us in history. and set before us the open but narrow door into his kingdom. To accept his Kingdom and enter in brings blessedness, because the best conceivable thing is that we should be in obedience to the will of God. Such

[1] Gustavo Gutierrez, *The Power of the Poor in History* (SCM Press, London, 1983), p.vii.
[2] C. H. Dodd, *The Parables of the Kingdom* (Nisbet & Co Ltd., London, 1935), p.50.
[3] *Ibid*, p.51.
[4] *Ibid*, p.198.

blessedness may be enjoyed here and now, but it is never exhausted in any experience that falls within the bounds of time and space.'[1]

Dodd maintains that the Old Testament prophets believed in a 'Day of the Lord', but that day has historically arrived, and a radical change has occurred between that age and this age through the death and resurrection of our Lord Jesus Christ.[2]

A good number of Christians in the Evangelical world are diametrically opposed to the view that the Kingdom of God has already been established. They see this world as hopelessly gripped in the claws of evil, and the only solution for this decadent society is the return of Christ in power and glory. This is the camp into which the NTCG traditionally falls. The present destabilization of world economy, barbaric acts of terrorism, decay in moral standards and ethical behaviour in this modern society, as it was in the days of Noah (Gen. 6.5-7), only undergird the belief that this world has reached the point of no return. The cry is 'even so come Lord Jesus'. George Eldon Ladd declares:

'The purpose of Jesus' earthly ministry was to bring God's Kingdom to man (Matt. 12.28). Because the King has come, we have already been delivered from the power of darkness and transferred into his Kingdom (Col. 1.13) . . . But his present reign is invisible, unseen, unrecognized by the world, visible only to the eye of faith. The order of the Age to Come will involve a new heaven and a new earth, and will be so different from the present order that we can speak of it as beyond history (2 Pet. 3.12; Rev. 21-22). The millenium will reveal to the world as we now know it the glory and power of Christ's reign.'[3]

The Gospels indicate that the announcement of the advent of the Kingdom of God broke suddenly upon a Roman-controlled world. Those who believed it proclaimed it, lived it and were even prepared to lay down their lives for it. According to Doctor Luke in the fourth chapter of his Gospel, it all began when a Stranger from Galilee sat in a Synagogue in Nazareth, and read from the book of Isaiah, chapter 61, 'The Spirit of the Lord is upon me because He has anointed me to preach the good news to the poor. He has sent me to proclaim release to the captives, and recovering of sight to the blind, to set at liberty those who are oppressed, to proclaim the acceptable year the Lord.' Jesus then turned to the people, calmly and unpretentiously announced, 'Today this Scripture has been fulfilled in your hearing' (Luke 4.17-25).[1]

In the opinion of Norman Gottwald, the passage in Isaiah was '. . . Setting forth an ecstatic announcement of the pending, but still delayed, redemption of Zion when more exiles are to be gathered, the nations will contribute to the cult of Yaweh, and peace and righteousness will flourish without limit.'[4] The writer of Isaiah was referring to the time when the wicked leaders would be cast

---

[1] Ibid, pp.209, 210.
[2] C. H. Dodd, *Apostle Preaching and Its Development* (Harper & Row, New York, 1964), p.80.
[3] George Eldon Ladd, *The Meaning of Millenium* Ed. Robert G. Glouse (Intervarsity Press, Illinois, 1977), p.39.
[4] Norman K. Gottwald, *The Hebrew Bible* (Fortress Press, Philadelphia, 1985), p.506.

out of office by the faithful servants of Yahweh' (Isa. 65.1-16); a re-created Jerusalem will be realized in the midst of a new heaven and new earth' (65.17-25), and Jewish exiles and foreigners will be gathered in. These will in turn herald the glory of Yahweh among the nations (66. 10-24).[1]

To the astonished crowd Jesus had declared that that day had arrived. The long-awaited promise was now fulfilled as God has established the relationship with his people. The Gentiles will see the glory of God and righteousness would spring forth among them. Jesus' life and work testified to his claim in so much that they at one time attempted to make him King by force (John 6.15). When later he hung dead upon the Roman cross, it was not only an enigma to his followers, but the laughing-stock of the Jews. To his closest friends all hope had gone. But Sunday came, and he burst forth from the tomb. God had vindicated his Son by raising him from the dead. They attested that this was 'according to the Scriptures.'[2] This good news shocked the hearers from Caesar's palace to the most humble dwelling in Palestine. Michael Green observes:

'There was no less joy on earth after the resurrection had set God's seal on the authenticity of Jesus. His disciples audaciously and exultantly spread this good news of a Saviour . . .. Sometimes we read that they spread the good news to people, Jew and Samaritan, Greek and Roman, bond and free.'[3]

It was natural to expect that the proclamation of the Kingdom in the sense in which Jesus announced it would have brought trouble on his followers, because it was seen to be an attack on the Roman Empire as it did at Thessalonica when Jason and the group that accepted Paul's good news were arrested (Acts 17.5-9).

In time, the early believers began to perceive Jesus as the embodiment of the kingly rule of God. Paul wrote to the Colossians, '. . . for in Christ the Godhead in all its fulness dwells incarnate,'[4] Michael Green notes that it was Origen, one of the early fathers who said, 'Jesus was the autobasileia, the kingdom in person.'[5] His life, his works, his death and resurrection, his Lordship became the substance of the apostolic proclamation. To them everything was Jesus. It seemed quite in order for them to proclaim Jesus as the good news of the Kingdom. As Mark states, 'Jesus came. . . preaching the kingdom of God is at hand.' (Mark 1.14-15) In other words, the appearance of Jesus brought within reach of all humanity the Kingdom of God. That Kingdom, observes Olando Costas,

'. . . is an indication of God's transforming presence in history. . .. The Kingdom stands for a new order of life: the new humanity and the new creation which have become possible through the death and resurrection of Jesus. This new order includes reconciliation with God, neighbour and nature, and therefore participation in a new world. It involves freedom from the power of sin and death, and consequently, the strength to live for God

---

[1] *Ibid*, p.507.
[2] Acts 2.21-27; 1 Cor. 15.4.
[3]. Michael Green, *Evangelism in the Early Church* (William B. Eerdmans Pub. Co., Grand Rapids, 1970), p.50.
[4] The Twentieth Century New Testament.
[5] Michael Green, *Evangelism in the Early Church*, p.51.

and humanity. It encompasses the hope of a more just and peaceful moral order, and thus it is a call to vital engagement in the historical struggle for justice and peace.'[1]

Costas continues to express that the transforming work of the Kingdom has an eschatological reality in that, though it has begun there is still a final consummation in history. He quotes J. Verkuyl as saying:

'The Kingdom of which the New Testament speaks has an incomparable depth and richness. It has dimensions which embrace heaven and earth, world history and the cosmos (cf. Colossians and Ephesians). The Kingdom of God is the new order which began in Christ and which will be completed by him, wherein all relationships will be put right, and not only that between God and man but also those between people, nations, sexes, generations and races, and between man and nature. It is this of which the prophets of Israel speak. This is the meaning of the visions in the book of Revelation. And it is this of which the apostles testify when they speak of looking forward to a new heavens and a new earth where justice dwells' (2 Pet. 3.13).[2]

Costas notes with regret that many Christians have not paid much attention to the message of the Kingdom. They have either over-emphasized its future consummation or supposed that it had failed to be the central concern of the gospel by the death and resurrection of our Lord. It is my opinion that some members of the NTCG have fallen into the former. The NTCG sees the only hope for the age is in the Second Coming of Christ to reign on earth a thousand years before the final consummation of all things, and the introduction of the new age.

In not too recent times, the struggle of Black people in the United States of America and Third World peoples, demanded a theological reflection on the dealing of God and his concern for the poor and oppressed. Thus Black Theology in the USA and Liberation Theology in Latin America were born. Referring to Black eschatology as seen by the African American people, Gayraud Wilmore observes:

'It was the acquaintance of Afro-American people with a "fight for life", with the experience of suffering and struggle that gave them an eschatology that took the message of liberation in the Old and New Testaments and welded them to the base of an African spirituality and to fading but still vital elements of the African World view. The result was a new eschatological perspective for Christianity in America. It arose in the sanctuary as the ecstasy of a vision of paradise at one moment, and in the next it drove believers into the streets to give that vision material actuality in the structure of society. In the worship experience of the black congregation Jesus Christ came every Sunday as the guarantor of a new reality "for all God's children—bringing to naught the things that are and bringing into existence the things that do not yet exist".' (1 Cor. 1.28)'.

---

[1] Orlando Costas, *The Integrity of Missions* (Harper & Row Pub., San Francisco, 1979), p.6.
[2] *Ibid*, pp.6, 7.
[3] Gayraud S. Wilmore, *Last Things First* (The Westminster Press, Philadelphia, 1982), p.161.

This was possible as the African world-view does not see a future apart from the present. Even the dead, in the world-view of the African, are present with us.

It can therefore be understood why Martin Luther King Jr., himself an African American, although brought up steeped in Baptist theology, could capture the ideas of the Black world-view and motivate Black people in their eschatological hope. It was not only a hope of the Kingdom of God as 'liberation from sin, slavery, and second-class citizenship, but also as freedom from bigotry, hatred, and alienation of people from one another in the land of their birth and common destiny.'[1]

Today, when some NTCG members reflect on the Black American experience, they consider what could be gleaned from it as they anticipate the growing struggle for survival among British-born Blacks and other Black settlers in Europe.

Liberation Theology which was born purely from a Roman Catholic movement in response to the spirit of Vatican II (1962-1965), called into question much of the traditional approach to theology which was seen as coming out of the comfortable libraries of the better privileged of the Christian community. It called for new strategies, social adjustments, and political struggle, being assisted by the prophetic elements in the Old Testament. Liberation Theology was sustained by popular religious opposition to consolidation of capitalist social processes. It is, in part, anti-imperialist Christian mode of thought and action. The Protestant process theologian John Cobb claimed:

> 'The greatest event in twentieth-century Church history was the Second Vatican Council. The greatest achievement which this event has made possible is the liberation theology and praxis of Latin America. In this event and this achievement freedom has won a victory.'[2]

This type of theology brings together the liberals and radicals. Here, conversion is understood as deliverance from conditions of political and economic bondage. Being born again is to be initiated into the struggle for a new world order. One of the exponents of this theology declares:

> 'The real Easter is not commemorative rhetoric. It is praxis; it is historical involvement . . .. I only experience rebirth at the side of the oppressed by being born again with them in their process of liberation.'[3]

This view totally alienates the spiritual implications of the doctrine of salvation and focuses on the political and material. It is a fact that in our world, people are facing oppression, exploitation and injustices, even at the hands of some Churches. Millions of oppressed people in South America and South Africa are brutalized and dehumanized by those who feel that God has given them the right to do so. And, in the case of South Africa, churchgoers who supported the extremists in seeking to maintain the evil Apartheid system that has destroyed the lives of millions are equally guilty. But, the tremendous contribution of church

---

[1] *Ibid*, p.89.
[2] Quoted in *Third World Book Review* Vol 1, No 4/5, 1985.
[3] Paulo Freire, 'Education, Liberation and the Church' in Alister Kee (ed.) *A Reader in Political Theology*, (Westminster Press, Philadelphia, 1974), p.100.

leaders and members who risked their lives and led protest marches, are worthy of praise. After years of torture and massacre of innocent lives, there now looms a ray of hope for the troubled masses in South Africa.

However, to consider the Easter message merely in terms of revolutionary engagements for physical liberation in the face of such injustices is greatly missing the point. For some, the process of consciousness-raising and radicalization has led to an extreme stance on liberation. They have forgotten that God has said, 'vengeance is mine, I shall repay.' Bloesch quite rightly takes to task Pannenberg who regards salvation as the coming kingdom, not as a supernatural intervention into history, but the natural destiny of the present society.[1]

Johannes Metz also perceives an eschatological outlook of the Church's hope (ultimate salvation) as 'emerging' and 'arising' in the here and now. He advocates a militant eschatology that would overthrow all oppressive structures by force. He would express his stance in such forceful statements as:

'Our eschatological expectation does not look for the heavenly-earthly Jerusalem as that ready-made and existing city of God. This heavenly city does not lie ahead of us as a distant hidden goal, which only needs to be revealed. The eschatological city of God is now coming into existence, for our hopeful approach builds this city. We are workers building this future, and not just interpreters of this future. The power of God's promises for the future moves us to form this world into the eschatological city of God.'[2]

This is obviously a very humanistic approach to accomplish the plan of God for the world. All efforts of men to do this have historically been a failure. A typical example is the recent denunciation of the Communistic system which had its strangle-hold on the Eastern European countries. Communism was once perceived as the hope for the poor and oppressed of our world, but the system has dismally failed Eastern European countries and other nations of the world.

From the foregoing, it is clear that the NTCG is faced with the dilemma of maintaining its theological position, which is chiliasm or millenarianism, and premillenarianism for that matter, and seek to conceptualize this theology in the face of present pressures being forced upon it. The NTCG can no longer remain asleep in the midst of the violence on our streets. Yet, at the same time, to jump on the 'bandwagon' of theologies that see no other hope for the future than politics and economics, would be a more daunting road to follow. It would seem that help could be found in Dodd and Ladd. Indeed the Kingdom has come, but the fullness is yet to be revealed at Christ's Second Coming.

The NTCG must uphold the Biblical mandate to preach the gospel, for only in so doing would the church maintain its evangelical vision. But it must also now look at the implications of this gospel; not only in spiritual terms, but in the basic literal principles of human life and experience. It was Jesus himself who taught the disciples to pray, 'Give us this day our daily bread', thus setting forth for all times, that humankind needs daily sustenance; that it was to be the concern of the Heavenly Father, and thus the concern of the Church. No area of human life

---

[1] Donald Bloesch, *Essentials of Evangelical Theology* Vol. 2 (Harper & Row Pub., New York, 1978), p.176.

[2] *Ibid*, Metz, Quoted in Bloesch, p.177.

is outside the parameter of Christ's concern, The same Christ that forgives sins, provides bread and fish to those who need them most. The over-spiritualization of areas of the gospel that ministered to human physical needs was part of the colonial theology practised by those who had never experienced the dehumanizing nature of slavery; hence they could not conceive of the necessity for present physical emancipation.

In some ways, it might be that Martin Luther King Jr. and the Black Church in America found some means of incorporating the hope of liberation from the humiliation of slavery and economic oppression, with the hope and themes of liberation from sin, and the hope of a better life. Perhaps it was all part of their unconscious African philosophy which makes no strict distinction between the spiritual and secular, or past, present or future. For as Noel Erskine observes:

'The awareness of . . . the despised and rejected one in its midst enabled the Black Church to become the inspirational source, the organizational drive, the sustaining power for a movement that might have faltered and failed but for the conviction that Almighty God himself was committed to the struggle and would reward those who endure to the end.'[1]

Certainly, if God were in the midst of his people, his eyes would be upon the righteous and his ears open to their cry for deliverance from oppression. The projection of deliverance from oppression into a distant future was quite in order for Western theology, as long as the Christian slave-owners would not be deprived of their slaves and the disruption of their economy. But for many Black slaves, who realized that they could not be delivered from their oppression, it was too bitter a thought to be endured and so they became alienated from the White man's theology and some deserted the Church altogether. Others developed and found comfort in Black Theology, Black religion and the Black Church. For the socially depressed Blacks, there was no difference between the cry for bread and the cry for forgiveness from sin and evil. A typical spiritual song entreats:

'O Lord, I'm hungry, I want to be fed;
O Lord, I'm hungry, I want to be fed;
O feed me, Jesus, Feed me;
Feed me all my day.
O Lord, I'm sinful, I want to be saved;
O Lord, I'm sinful, I want to be saved;
O save me, Jesus, Save me,
Save me all my days.'[1]

It must not be forgotten that the hope of the gospel is not only for forgiveness from sin, but for a new life. Jesus came that we might have life and that we may have it more abundantly (Jn. 10.10). The Church will do well to rethink its theology to be more attuned to the cry of the hopeless, and distressed, and enable them to live with the tension of the times while responding to the tension of the eschaton. For truly, for those who are in Christ, the Kingdom has come.

---

[1] Noel Erskine, *Decolonizing Theology* (Orbis Books, Maryknoll, New York, 1981), pp.55, 56.

[2] *Ibid*, p.57, quoted from James H. Cone, The Spirituals and Blues (Seabury, New York, 1972), p.51.

6. Gospel in Action

From the exploration of the working of the New Testament Church of God over the past 35 years of its establishment and the plight of the African-Caribbean people in Britain, there was no doubt in the minds of the members of the Site Team that this was the time for some action to demonstrate the liberating effect of the gospel. This action was not just to be a reaction to a set of issues or injustices that were evident in society, but rather a response rooted in theology to direct the Church in this area of social action. Edward Wimberly was correct when he observed that Black pastoral care should be in terms of Christian understanding of the gospel message and the willingness to serve others as a result. He argued that,

> 'Numerous Black Christians have understood the gospel in terms of liberation of persons from oppressive forces in society. Some thinkers see liberation in terms of freeing the oppressed by a radical transformation of social and political structures. Others see liberation as needed not only in the social and political arena, but also in the lives of individuals—the freeing of the self . . . For our purposes, then, liberation as a norm . . . refers to the freeing of persons from those internal and external forces that prevent them from moving toward their full potential as self- actualizing, assertive human beings related to God.'[1]

The Team recognized that the Church, apart from endeavouring to look after the spiritual life of the membership, had failed to enable members and those in its community to develop their full potential and live out their Christian life in the full context of the liberating power of the gospel. To correct this situation, it was felt that action should be effected to increase the involvement of the NTCG in responding to the social and economic situation. After consideration of several suggestions, it was agreed that this can best be achieved by:

A. The setting up of a Department of Social Responsibility
B. Developing Co-operation between African Caribbean people.

Part A. *The Setting up of a Department of Social Responsibility*

(a) MINISTERIAL SANCTION

As there was no such Department in the natural structure of the Church, it was necessary to have a systemic change; such a change required the sanction of the Ministry of the NTCG. At a meeting of the National Executive Council of the NTCG held on 18 September, 1986, the findings of the Site Team were presented and the project of setting up a Department of Social Responsibility was discussed. The project received the approval of the Executive Council and this cleared the way for its presentation to the District Overseers[2] on 19 September

---

[1] Edward P. Wimberly, *Pastoral Care in the Black Church* (Abingdon Press, Nashville, 1979), p.74.

[2] These are senior ministers acting in an administrative role over a number of Churches. The geographical boundaries of a District are determined by the National Overseer.

1986. They too welcomed the proposal as it revealed the wide range of opportunities for further ministry. Some pastors had already made application to their local Councils for assistance; others had clubs for the elderly and play-groups operating at their Churches. However, the majority had no idea of what could be done. The NTCG had not undertaken such social programmes and those pastors who ran clubs or play-groups did so without official endorsement.

On Saturday 20 September 1986, at the National Ministers' Conference, the proposal for a Department of Social Responsibility was presented. The Ministry was informed that it had already had the approval of the Executive Council and District Overseers. It was then being presented to the entire body of ministers for adoption. The plan for the department and its function were outlined and explained, and after much discussion it was unanimously accepted by the Conference. In order that a co-ordinated programme could be possible throughout the branch Churches, the NTCG Department of Social Responsibility aimed to launch a National Community Action Programme. The aim of the programme was to:

(a) create employment
(b) provide a very high standard of training in areas of Computer Programming, Book-keeping and Accounts.
(c) provide a wide range of facilities and services for the following,
  i. Senior Citizens—sheltered accommodation for the Elderly at the Main House, Overstone Park.
  ii. Under-fives Creche
  iii. Disabled
  iv. The Unemployed
  v. One-parent families
  vi. Orphans

The target group were to be people living in Council estates in areas of high unemployment and those which were generally regarded as disadvantaged, or handicapped, in urban priority areas.

To meet the objectives of the Department, centres throughout the nation would have to be established. Local Churches with adequate space and appropriate facilities would be regarded as the 'Centres.'

At the centres a number of programmes such as the following sample would be developed:

Mornings
(a) Senior Citizens Club
(b) Small woodwork workshops
(c) Small Art and Craft workshops
(d) Designing and Dressmaking workshops
(e) Counselling and advice sessions: drugs, health, welfare rights, marriage etc.
(f) Book-keeping, accounts and computer courses

	(g)	Evening Adult Literacy courses
Evenings	(h)	Homework studies
	(i)	Youth and Recrxeation club
	(j)	Art and drama sessions
	(k)	Music
	(l)	Home visits: Elderly, One-parent
	(m)	Street mission (providing food for tramps (etc.)

	(n)	Supplementary Schools
Saturdays	(o)	Orphanage visits and trips Big Brother Scheme (Youths visiting orphans and taking them out)
	(p)	Remand Home Visit programme

It would be the responsibility of the Regional and District Managers to ensure that these activities are planned to meet the demands of the particular region.

The staffing structure of the Department, for the time being, was as set out in Figure (i) and the Duties of the Officers and operation of the department were as set out in Appendix 3. It was to be noted that all the officers appointed were to work voluntarily and funding would be sought for full-time support for those unemployed.

Figure 1

DEPARTMENT OF SOCIAL MINISTRY

NTCG NATIONAL COMMUNITY PROJECT

MANAGEMENT STRUCTURE

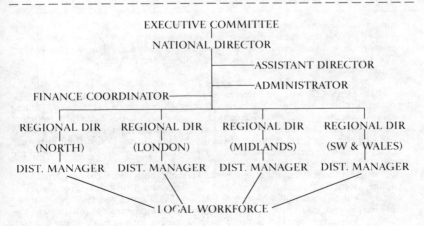

(b) CONTACTS AND AGENCIES

Essential to the setting up of the Department was the location of possible areas of funding. One of the Site Team members came in contact with Michael Hastings who at that time was undertaking a feasibility study for the Department of Employment on the eight Priority Areas where government had plans for assisting ethnic minority groups to develop projects. The NTCG had churches in seven of the eight Priority Areas[1] and, as such, Hastings was a valuable contact. A meeting was arranged with him at Overstone on Wednesday 24 September, with Eric Brown and Rudolph Parkinson (Site Team Members) present. Hastings was highly impressed by the Church's proposed initiative in the area of social ministries, and was introduced to the new programme that was about to be launched. It was felt that the Department, fully established, could serve as the Agency through which Government could channel funds for the projects in branches of the church throughout the nation.

Following this meeting, another consultation was held at Hasting's office on 18 November, when the report of his findings throughout the nation was discussed. At this consultation were Philip Mohabir, of African-Caribbean Evangelical Alliance and Clive Calver, General Secretary of the Evangelical Alliance. Michael's Report was to be presented to the then Secretary of State for Employment and he had mentioned in it the positive contribution of Black-led Churches and the NTCG in particular in the Inner Cities. As a result of these contacts, later that year, two very important engagements were accomplished.[2] These were to have positive effects on the NTCG and open up opportunities for the involvement of the Church in greater community affairs.

(c) LAUNCHING OF THE PROJECT

A letter was sent to all the District Overseers announcing the selection of personnel to the various offices of the Department and requesting the District Over-

---

[1] Priority Areas seem to be areas of high level of unemployment, especially among ethnic minorities, and that apparently have had riots, or which through poor housing and economic conditions require urgent government assistance. These were: Brixton, Peckham (London), Leicester, Handworth (Birmingham), Moss Side (Manchester), Bristol, Middlesborough, and Chapeltown (Leeds).

[2] My wife and I were invited to a Reception at 10 Downing Street, by the Prime Minister and Mr. Dennis Thatcher on 1 December 1986. We had the opportunity to talk about the work of the Church with the Prime Minister who expressed an interest in learning more about the work of Black-led Churches in the Inner Cities. Regretfully, much of the work of the Churches in ministering to the needs of the poor and marginalized is not well publicized. The number of youths that have been rescued from drugs and other vices, and whose lives have been transfromed continues to be a credit to the social work of the Church.

I was also a member of the group that had consultations with Kenneth Clarke M.P., at the Home Office on 9 December 1986. This group included Clive Calver of Evangelical Alliance, Philip Mohabir of African-Caribbean Evangelical Alliance and Michael Hastings. The proposal for the Evangelical Enterprise was presented and discussed at that meeting. This project was subsequently funded to aid in the development of projects in the Inner cities.

seers to serve as District Managers or appoint someone in their place.[1] A meeting of all those appointed was held on 22 November 1986 and the Department of Social Responsibility was launched at Overstone. Arnold Kirlew was appointed as Director. It was his responsibility to make applications to various funding agencies so as to attract funding for the national project. For the time being, the offices of Administrative Assistant and Accountant were to be handled from the National Overseer's Office, and the Church's Accountant at headquarters (Overstone) until funding for these offices could be organized. (Unfortunately, up to this time funds have not been found for this purpose).

The launching of the project was well received by all those who attended. The discussion revealed the depth of concern that members had for the social needs of the members of the Church and community—especially those of senior citizens. It was felt that this programme was long overdue and that no effort should be left unturned to ensure the success of the Department. One District Overseer, Cecil Fisher, presented a copy of an interim report prepared by a student at Leicester Polytechnic for the Social Services Committee on the needs of African Caribbean Elderly in the Leicester area. This report revealed a great need for caring in this sector of the community, and highlighted the necessity for an agency such as the NTCG Department of Social Responsibility to help meet those needs. The national Director was advised to arrange an early meeting of the District Managers to review the projects that could be undertaken in various areas and to assist in writing proposals for submission by January 1987.

Part B. *Developing Co-operation between African Caribbeans*

The second change goal was endeavouring to sensitize the African Caribbean people to the benefits of working in co-operation with each other. The need was evidenced by the fragmentation that existed even among the Black-led Churches themselves. The appeal for co-operation was to be brought before them through a programme of Biblical and theological analysis, coupled with a project requiring joint effort by Church members in a needy area.

STRATEGIES FOR CHANGE

The theme for the NTCG for the year 1987 was 'Covenant to Care.' This was chosen so as to enable the entire organization to reflect theologically and Biblically on the concept of co-operation through caring. Subsequently, at seminars, conventions and general Church services the focus was on caring. It was important to emphasize that there must be a sense of caring for each other to foster co-operation in the home, Church and community. This fact is becoming even more crucial as we move into 1992 and the challenges of a new European order.

The Book of Nehemiah was found to be very helpful in projecting this theme. An encyclical entitled 'Look to Yourselves and Unto God' was sent to all pastors to be read to the Churches. It was based on Nehemiah 2.18, and Nehemiah 3. Other texts that were used from time to time were: Ps. 133.3; Luke 5.4-7; John 17.20, 21; Acts 4.32; 1 Cor. 10.16; 12.12, and 1 Peter 3.8.

---

[1] In most cases District Overseers would serve as the District Managers, but the intention is to replace them by lay persons with suitable qualifications for community work.

My wife, Muriel Joyce, as President of the Department for Ladies Ministries chose 'Responsibility to Care' as the theme for the Ladies' activities. At their October Regional Seminars held at Highgate, Birmingham, and Brixton, London, the opportunity was given to project the benefits of co-operative action in caring. The Reverend F. A. Beason, then the pastor of the largest NTCG church in Jamaica, and Radio Minister for the organization there, was invited as a featured speaker for the two weekend seminars. He presented three sermons on the Good Samaritan, Luke 10.30-37, emphasizing the basic idea that co-operation was brought about when believers demonstrated care and compassion; but insularity and selfishness were the termites that destroyed co-operation and fellowship. Over four thousand people attended the Seminars and received sound Biblical analyses throughout the three-day events.

Efforts were not only made to bestir the members, it was found that co-operation was also lacking among ministers. A seminar was therefore organized in July 1987. Among those who addressed the ministry were Michael Hastings of Evangelical Enterprise, and Arnold Kirlew. These speakers challenged the ministers to recognize the potential that exists in an organization such as ours, both in size and resources to affect the nation if it could motivate its membership to more co-operative activities. In time, there developed among the ministers a readiness to see some co-operative business set up by the Church and our Solicitors were instructed to explore such possibilities having regard to the Aims and Objectives of the Memorandum of Association of the NTCG as a Registered Company limited by guarantee.

The co-operative ventures that were considered were in the areas of providing goods and services to the Church as a whole; purchasing, repairing and refurbishing old buildings to provide accommodation for the needy, and employment for the unemployed. It was also envisaged that te company could handle or manage contracts for the repair to NTCG buildings, some over one hundred years old.

CO-OPERATION AMONG OTHER ETHNICS

It was commonly acknowledged that there was not enough co-operation among Black people and this was a contributory factor to their lack of economic progress on a whole. It was therefore agreed that a visit should be made to an Asian community project to see what could be learnt from that society whose success in business in this country was evidenced by their togetherness as an ethnic minority.

A visit was made to a Pakistani community project in Birmingham. In answer to questions concerning the key to the co-operativeness among that community, the leader who had come to England at the age of 14 and had experienced the pressures of growing up in this society, felt that co-operation among them grew out of three distinctives:
1. language and culture
2. religion
3. extended family system

He stressed the importance of identity in any society, and saw that these distinctives were the carriers of their identity and the basis of their togetherness. He was asked whether a white community leader could enhance the co-operation among their people. He quickly responded:

'No! No! That's what happened before I came in. My predecessor had a good intention, but he was not able to communicate because it is not just the language, it is understanding of the culture. For instance, if a person walks in, even an angry person, I stand up and I go and shake hands and greet him. With regards to women, when it is the women's group, I do not enter because I know that there is certain culture, respect, understanding and behaviour which I must adopt.'[1]

The leader then emphasized the role his religion had in unifying his people. He felt it was more important to him to be identified as a Moslem, rather than a Pakistani, or British. He sadly alluded to the fact that their faith was being heavily eroded among their young people, and he blamed the State school system. See Appendix 4

From this interview, one concluded that the African Caribbean people needed to find some unifying agent and it was suggested that the NTCG could be that agent. Contrary to common ideas, African Caribbean people do not all have the same culture, for they did not all originate from the same tribes of Africa; nor were they acculturated by the same Colonial experience. However, education and common destiny have caused them to recognize the fact that they must come together as Black people if only for the means of survival.

It is gratifying to observe that there is a lot more understanding and co-operation today among the younger generation of British-born Blacks, and, to a large extent more unity among Caribbean governments as a greater degree of Black consciousness is realized, and the Colonial chains have been broken.

The following are examples of projects that were started since the Church took on greater emphasis in Social Responsibility and the efforts to stimulate co-operation among the African Caribbean people.

Part C. *Birmingham Experience*
Birmingham is the second largest city in England. In the height of the industrial boom, Birmingham was the place for people to find jobs in factories and industries requiring manual and semi-skilled labour. It was no surprise therefore, that Birmingham had more than its fair share of immigrants. Now that the industrial life of the city has long since declined, it has become a place of very high unemployment, especially among Blacks (See Table of Unemployment).

As many African Caribbean people flocked to Birmingham in the fifties and sixties, the NTCG established many churches in this area. There are also a good

---

[1] Mr. Majid claimed that his knowledge of and respect for the cultural values of his people helped him to elicit from them better co-operation than someone outside his culture would receive. To the average worker outside his culture, behaviour would have to be conducted according to the norms and values of the dominant culture. Those were some of the sociological factors that were so commonly overlooked in an ethnocentric community when dealing with black people.

number of other Black-led Churches, some being offshoots of the main groups due to administrative and other power struggles.

The New Testament Church of God prided itself as being one of the first groups to start in this area. As far back as 1952 attempts were made to gather small groups of Christians from Jamaica together by men like J. A. Johnson, Enus Gordon and others. However, their main concern had been to maintain the Church's exclusive message of repentance towards God and faith in our Lord Jesus Christ. Apart from aiding one another in finding accommodation very little was done in assisting the new immigrants to settle in this society. However, the situation now no longer remains the same; a new revolution has begun.

(1) Family Co-operative

For over five years E. A.Thomas, a member of the Muntz Street NTCG, Birmingham, had been burdened to see some co-operative action taken by the Church to facilitate the needs of the growing Black population in his area. In his own words, he spent many sleepless nights contemplating: 'What will happen to our African Caribbean people in this country within the next twenty to twenty-five years?' He felt some action was necessary on the part of the people themselves. He reckoned that if 1000 people saved ten pounds per week, that could realize £10,000. In fifty-two weeks they could realize £520,000. He then dreamed of 6,000 taking part, and saw the potential of £31,200,000 being realized.

Burning with his ideas, he contacted friends—Rev. D. Webley, Rev. C. Dennis, Messrs Sealy, Brown, Elliot, Walters and others. After a visit by the National Overseer to their church and, on learning of the work being done by the Department of Social Responsibility, E. A.Thomas was encouraged to pursue his plans as he felt that the NTCG was not averse to such community action.

With the help of a Community Outreach Project training officer, he was able to set up a meeting on 29 April 1986 out of which a Steering Committee was appointed to look more closely at his ideas and, occasionally, I was being informed of the progress of the work being done by the the committee. Support from the Church was seen as vital to the success of the venture. It was not the first time that Thomas had approached the leaders of the Church, but now that the Department of Social Responsibility was there to encourage such initiatives, he saw that as a support mechanism he had longed for. Several meetings were held at which the legal considerations were brought before the members. The final proposal was presented on the 29 September 1986 by the Steering Committee. The Constitution was that of an Industrial and Provident Society with alterations to suit the particular needs of the group. The name, Caribbean Co-operative Enterprise was adopted. The details of the proposal are set out in Appendix 5.

Unfortunately, now five years down the road, the project has not really grown as was anticipated. Reflecting on the success or failure of the project, one member of the Steering Committee noted that perhaps Thomas was too ambitious in his projections, and tried too hard without properly selling the ideas that burned within him. After a short illness some two weeks ago, Thomas passed away to be with the Lord. To many he was a trusted friend, brother and visionary. One thing

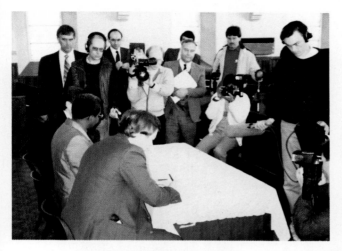

Mr. Kenneth Clarke, the Secretary of State for Trade and Industry signs the agreement in Leicester on 26 October 1986 (see pages 74 and 75).
(Pictures continued overleaf)

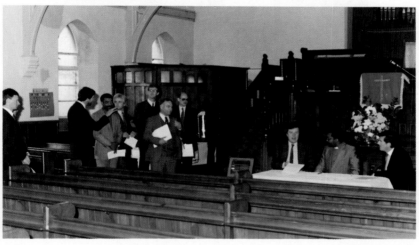

Captions on previous page

Overstone Park

Worship—officials and choir
Brighton Convention 1991

Brighton Convention 1991

did not fail, however, he lived to see the erection of a new church building; one of his most treasured dreams. A simple, yet profound man; one who believed in, and stood up for, a better and more co-operative spirit among his people. That was his life. In his death, he left behind a dream yet to be fulfilled. I am informed by one of the members that they are soon to meet to decide where they go from the place he led them.

(2) Handsworth NTCG Youth Training Scheme
In September 1985 there was a riot at Villa Road and Lozells Road, Handsworth, Birmingham. While the fire was raging at the old Cinema, and rioters looted the burning shops on the streets, about two hundred yards away, at the NTCG on Lozells and George Steet, the members were having a meeting, totally oblivious to what was going on outside. When the meeting was over and they tried to get home, they found that the streets around the Church were blocked off by Police. It was only then that they realized that a riot had taken place so close to them. This is a typical example of how the Church had over the years succeeded in keeping itself cut off from the happenings in the wider community.

I visited the area following the riot along with the National Secretary, Revd. R. H. Parkinson and the National Youth Director, Revd. E. Brown and met the Pastor S. U. Thompson. Together with other clergymen, we surveyed the damage of that night of rampage in which two members of the Asian community were burnt to death in their shop. We then returned to the Church were we found the members serving cups of tea and biscuits to scores of policemen who were deployed in the area to help keep the peace. Between their patrols they found this courtesy a welcoming respite from the cold.

Sometime following the aftermath of the riot, the (Anglican) Dean of Aston and Handsworth called for a forum of Black and White Churches in the Aston and Handsworth area to be formed. The Churches decided to approach Government for funds to support training for unemployed youngsters. It was the belief that joblessness, poor housing, poor education and powerlessness were some of the contributing factors to the riot. Youths wondered the street filled with despair, and with nothing worthwhile to do they became tools for those who thrive on making life uncomfortable for others.

Following this meeting of which Pastor Thompson was a part, he conferred with two young men of his Church on the likely action they could take at the NTCG, Handsworth. One of these young men was John Grey who had only recently attended the Ministers' Conference at which the Department of Social Responsibility was approved. He recalls that he was greatly challenged by the message preached by the Overseer in which he declared, 'We are God's answer to the cry of the suffering.' John was motivated to attempt a programme for training unemployed youth of Handsworth. He claimed, '... Because of the concept we have of how the Church views social action, one is very timid. But to hear that message coming from the leadership made me know where the Church is now going.'[1]

---

[1] Interview with John Grey held at the Project Site at George Street, Handsworth.

With the help of another member of the Church, Kenneth Rodney, John drew up a proposal to be presented to the Manpower Service Commission[1], but it was not favourably received. They then took the proposal to the Job Centre where they were instructed to present it to the Handsworth Task Force, about February 1987. They were then advised to solicit the help of an Anglican Vicar, David Collyer, in refining the proposal, which was then approved by the Task Force.

At first it was decided that £37,000 be spent on the Handsworth Church to refurbish rooms for the project. After discussion with the local officers of the Church, it was suggested that a vacant lot at the rear of the Church's premises could be used for the erection of a prefab building with office space of 2500 square feet for the project at a cost of £40,000. This was accepted by the Task Force and the Handsworth Breakthrough company was chosen to receive the funding and handle the construction. The Rev. David Collyer and The Rev. S. U. Thompson were Co-Chairman of the company of Directors. After completion John Grey was employed as the Director.

The project was in line with Government's Youth Training Scheme, providing Business training for 16- and 17-year-olds. It offered City and Guilds, Royal Society of Arts, Pitman and General Certificate or Education certificates in the following areas:

Computer training
Business Administration
Business Legal Studies
Short-hand/Typing
Office Practice
Reception Work
Marketing

John worked assiduously during the construction of the project which became the pride of the people in Handsworth. There was the feeling that at last the Church was waking up to the needs of the community and was making some positive contribution to the joblessness and lack of training in the area.

When the project was completed, the Task Force approved a grant for three years for the Director. The training was being assisted by ADM Company (now Cranbrook Training), a business training company situated in the city. They provided four teachers who were funded by the MSC. Part of the equipment supplied by the Task Force included 15 Amstrad 1512 computers, and 12 Olympia electronic typewriters.

John used the centre for seminars to train others on weekends on courses in computer and business in order to introduce more professionalism into Black business and services. He also planned to make space available to the Industrial Society to run courses there[2]. With a deep sense of satisfaction John explained

---

[1] (MSC) Manpower Service Commission was a government agency providing funding for community projects for unemployed and other voluntary agencies. It operated under the Department of Employment.

[2] Industrial Society is a Council with Royal Patronage, as the Duke of Edinburgh is the patron. The Industrial Society has the support of senior people in all areas of industry, commerce, the public service and trade unions. Their headquarters are located at Peter Rouge House, 3 Carlton House Terrace, London SW17 3DS.

that the project was seeking to train youth before they could be spoilt by the gangs on the streets. He also noted that he could walk into the shops where the drug-pushers were hanging out and would be recognized as someone from the Church who was making a difference in the community.

But, alas, the success was short-lived. Power struggle over the running of the Scheme developed after one year. Even though the project had trainees from the African Caribbean, Asian and Chinese communities, and there were evidences of success in their achievements, complaints were levelled against John's administration by those over him. This led to the Rev. S. U. Thompson resigning from the Chairmanship of the Company as moves were made to remove John from his position, and the project from the control of the Church that had invested so much, in terms of land space and other facilities.

Efforts to negotiate a reasonable settlement proved futile and the Rev. S. U. Thompson was forced to ask the Handsworth Breakthrough to cease operation on the Church's premises. The project was moved to rented accommodation on the Soho Road leaving the prefab office block on the Church's land.

There was still the burning desire of the Church to carry out the project as originally envisioned and so approaches were made to the Task Force to permit the Church to purchase the prefab office block that was still on its premises, and for which no rent or compensation was paid to the Church. The Task Force refused stating that the agreement with Handsworth Breakthrough and the Secretary of State for Trade and Industry required that any resources left behind since Handsworth Breakthrough no longer used the premises should be returned to the Task Force. Further, as the Task Force was closing down in Handsworth, the resource was to be re-allocated to the East Birmingham Task Force, and be gifted to another Scheme.

Pastor Thompson and I along with two other leaders went to the East Birmingham Task Force office to explain the Church's position on the whole transaction for we expected that the Church would be considered, even from a moral and ethical standpoint considering the damage the removal of the project from the Church's premises had caused to the morale and goodwill exercised by all in the initial development of the project. In addition, the cost to Government of dismantling the building and making good the site could have been compensated by their acceptance of the Church's offer to purchase the building. But it seemed that there were forces that were determined to see that no good should come out of it.

It was generally felt that the behaviour of the Breakthrough leadership did not augur well for better cooperation between Black-led and White Church initiatives in the area. A sad fact that had to be contemplated by both Black and White leaders who were sympathetic to the project. However, it is hoped that time and God will heal all.'

NEW VISION

Out of the ashes of despair over the closure of the project came a new vision for the future. Had this affair not been dealt with expeditiously by pastor

Thompson, serious disturbances could have arisen in the area. However, sound common sense and spiritual maturity led away from friction to new action. Efforts were made by John to turn the stumbling stones into building blocks and STEPS (Spiral Training and Employment Personnel Service) was launched at the NTCG Church hall on 18 March, 1991. There in the spacious hall were exhibitors from the City: British Gas, West Midlands Electric, Cadburys, Rover, Royal Mail, West Midlands Fire, West Midlands Police, IMI, TSB, Sainsburys, John Carter Ltd, and City Colleges. The convention was scheduled to introduce school-leavers to vocations offered in the City. The Personnel Director of West Midlands Electric, Mr Colin Evans, addressed the crowds after I had opened with prayer and declared the convention opened.

Between 11.00 a.m. and 3.00 p.m. youngsters from the schools and colleges passed through the halls receiving information and being interviewed by representatives from the different organizations. From 5.00 p.m. till 9.00 p.m., parents and other members of the community dropped in. It is estimated that about 750 persons (students and people from the community) passed through the hall and received information on opportunities in the city. Blacks; Whites and Asians had nothing but praise for the convention. John is still optimistic that the Church might have an opportunity to erect facilities to carry out the much-needed training for Handsworth.

Part D. *Leicester on the Move*
The Leicester NTCG is situated in Highfields, the Black and Asian heartland of Leicester. This was one of the Government priority areas of the Inner City. It has gained notoriety because of high unemployment and the riots that erupted there in 1985. The Black population is not very high in Leicester, but yet there is a high rate of economically inactive Blacks in that area. This perhaps is not uncommon for other areas of many Inner Cities of Britain today.

The NTCG has owned a building in Leicester since 1964, but as far as can be ascertained, there has been nothing done in the area of social concern for the needy people of this community. Apart from seeking to rescue those perishing in sin, the Church left those perishing materially to the fate of their relatives or Government Agencies.

In 1986, the new pastor, the Rev. Cecil E. Fisher, began to share his concern for the Elderly and Youths in his Church. At the launching of the Department of Social Responsibility, he was made District Manager for Social Responsibility in his area. This opened for him the opportunity to put flesh to some of the ideas he had for the needs of his people.

He wrote a proposal as outlined in Appendix 8 and after discussing this with the me, he submitted it to the City Council for a Capital grant of £60,000 to enable him to set up a Senior Citizen's Club, Under-fives and Youth Club. This application was turned down; but the pastor was not discouraged. He believed that there was a genuine need in the Highfields area for something to be done to tackle the high unemployment among the youth and ease the tension that existed there. His faith was soon to be rewarded. Gratefully, he recalls:

'. . . Our God is big! I believe he touched the heart of Simon Pilling from the Government Task Force. I was in the Church office when Mr. Pilling rang to say that he had. seen the application I had submitted to the Council and believed that there could be some help if jobs and training would result from the programme for the people in the Highfields area.'[1]

The Church was later visited and an architect drew up the plan for the remodelling of the ground floor to provide the necessary facilities for training. Twenty-six persons from the Highfields area would be provided work and training for 10 months to a year. The trainees would be provided tools and training they would not ordinarily have had.

McAlpine was the firm that won the contract and they undertook the restoration and remodelling of the hall. A grant totalling £379,426 was made available by the Task Force for the project and the Secretary of State for Trade and Industry, Kenneth Clarke M.P., visited Leicester on 26 October to sign the Agreement with the NTCG. As National Overseer, I signed the Agreement on behalf of the Church. The pastor, Cecil Fisher, was overjoyed at the launching of the project and remarked that after the completion of the ten months project, a playgroup for Under-fives would be run at the Church. Already there were thirty children enrolled. There were also plans to create a training programme for youths in the community. 'Right now,' he remarked, 'we have 26 happy people working on the project. Some of them have not worked for over five years and some under.'[2]

It was reported that the foreman for McAlpine discovered by chance that one of the young men doing labouring had artistic skills. He inquired if anyone was able to do sign-writing as a display board had to be written for the project. The young man volunteered and did a good job. The foreman then went into the City and found a job for the lad at a printer's shop, a job he had never dreamed of before. This was one example of the fact that opportunities abound, if only one had the right connection.

Part E. *Overstone Developments*

As has been mentioned in an earlier chapter, the Overstone manor built over a hundred years ago for Lord Overstone (S Jones Loyd, a multi-millionaire Manchester banker), fell into the hands of the NTCG in 1980. This 116-room Victorian building designed by William M. Teulon, and planned around a beautiful hand-carved central staircase, and with the large and stately rooms with decorated ceilings, still displayed signs of grandeur and elegance, though it was derelict and in great need of repair.

---

[1] The Rev. Cecil Fisher could find no other words to define the magnificent turn of events. As District Manager for the Department of Social Responsibility, and as Pastor of the Local Church for that time, he applied for and obtained a grant for refurnishing the main hall, kitchen and offices to carry out a programme of social responsibility.

[2] Remarks from the Rev. Cecil Fisher, as he reflected on the blessings the Project had brought to the Community.

The previous owners, Overstone Girls' School had to abandon the premises after 50 years of the school's existence due to the high cost of repairs estimated at £250,000. The estate was split up and sold off to various private owners. Interestingly enough, the stables which used to house the horses were bought and converted into beautiful and luxurious flats. (One was on the market for over £200,000).

The purchase of Overstone by the Church was the vision of the Rev. J. McIntyre who saw its potential as a place to run a training Centre for the Youth of the Church; and, in due time, a retirement home for ministers. Not everyone shared his vision; but McIntyre was not a man to be daunted by obstacles. Like the famous missionary and explorer, Dr. William Carey, he would say, Attempt great things for God, and expect big things from God.'

This for him was a challenge to the Church to do something for posterity. Something that would symbolize the capacity of Black people in Britain. It would demonstrate that even though it was felt that Black folk were inadequate and incapable, they could transform a sore thumb' into a healthy and viable functioning structure. Secondly, to own land in what seemed to be a highly prized part of the country was, in itself, an achievement. This fact is borne out by the commonly asked question by visitors, 'How did you manage to buy in here?'

Support of Members

After four years of struggle, the General Officials of the Church felt that the crippling effects Overstone had on the national Church and ministry warranted the abandonment of the property. However, the grassroots members of the Church and some ministers would hear nothing of it. It was felt that help should be sought and proper plans made to make the building profitable.

A firm of consultants was called in to suggest ways in which Overstone could better be used as Headquarters for the NTCG, facilities for a Bible College, a Conference Centre and a Senior Citizen's home. After several meetings, the consultants requested £15,000 to do a feasibility study and prepare a brochure. It was felt at the time that the Church could not afford the funds.

The Daventry Council was approached, as the building is listed, but the response was not favourable. The MSC representatives visited and looked over the building, but no suitable project to link the premises with the community so as to attract the funding for the much-needed repairs could be found.

Approach was made to the Home Office and the Department of Environment, but this also led to a dead end. As the building had Grade II listing, an application was made to English Heritage[1] for help to treat dry rot and fungal decay but that also yielded no fruit.

When all doors seemed to be closed we received an invitation to attend a seminar conducted at the Community Service Volunteers (CSV) headquarters at Pentonville Road, London. At that meeting were other Black community leaders from various parts of the country. Ted Watkins of Watts Labour Coummunity

---

[1] English Heritage is a national society with responsibility for assisting in preserving buildings of architectural and historic value and works of art.

Action Committee (WLCAC), Watts, Los Angeles, California, USA was the speaker.

Ted Watkins explained that since the riots in Watts in 1965, where '. . . the city burned for days, hundreds were injured and killed, and people were left homeless,' there had not been another riot in Watts. He argued that through the creation of community enterprises, the people of Watts had ownership of assets (e.g., hospitals, garages, petrol stations, supermarkets, housing estates, etc.) and were thus able to identify with the area where they had been born and lived for years, and were motivated to build rather than to destroy. It seemed that ownership led to responsible action and a sense of self-worth in that community.

Following this meeting, members of the Site Team visited CSV for a meeting with B. Cunningham, then a WLCAC Development Worker in London. Further meetings were held with UK 2000 representatives. All these efforts led to the a project being submitted to City Parochial Foundation (Trust).

The Project was basically for the funding of a Researcher to do a feasibility study on the use of the 32 acres of land at Overstone by groups of Black-led organizations in London to design and develop enterprise ventures and so improve their economic potential. (For details of the project see Appendix 8). The project was accepted, and an Advisory Board was appointed. A Researcher was appointed after the post was advertised in the *Jamaica Gleaner* and he began his work in October 1987. At a later meeting of the Advisory Board, Janet Hatfield, CSV suggested that a Development worker should also be appointed to look at the possibility of further developments on the Overstone building and land. The office was to work closely with the Researcher so as to put into motion any work that seemed feasible while the Researcher was carrying out the study. For the Development worker, a grant was received from Barclays Bank Social Responsibility Unit.

The study was completed and submitted to the Advisory Board who successfully negotiated another grant from Barclays to assist in the implementation of the project. The Horticultural project got under way and has been running fairly successfully for the past two years. During the last financial year, as the project is involved in training youths, it attracted funding from the Department of Education and Science. So far, one student has completed his course and left the Scheme for other employment. The produce is successfully sold all around the country at the various Senior Citizens and Luncheon Clubs sponsored by the Church.

Senior Citizens' Respite

The prayer of the writer in Psalm 71. 17, 18, struck a resounding chord throughout the Church each time one considered the aged members of our congregation. The writer prayed:

'O God, thou hast taught me from my youth; and hitherto have I declared thy wondrous works. Now also when I am old and grey-headed, O God, forsake me not; until I have shewed thy strength unto this generation, and thy power to everyone that is to come.'

In the midst of the search for ways to make Overstone a viable operation, the focus was also on the possibility of part of the building being used as a Respite for Senior Citizens.

Joyce (my wife) and I were invited to attend a meeting of the Standing Conference for Ethnic Minority Senior Citizens (SCEMSC) in London November 1986. It was there that we came to realize what was being done in London through this Agency that serves as an umbrella for several Senior Citizens clubs. At that meeting were representatives from Black, Cypriot, Chinese, Asian and African communities. We came away determined to see that a proper plan be enacted to link the efforts being carried out to aid Senior Citizens in some of our Churches. At that time, clubs were being run at Brixton, Handsworth, Leeds, Wolverhampton and a few other churches, but no attempt was being made to co-ordinate the programmes. Everyone was struggling in one's own way to promote some sort of caring for the Elderly; some were successful in obtaining grants to build or refurbish halls to conduct their activities.

Joyce began writing letters to several Charities seeking help to repair part of the Overstone building for setting up of a home for the elderly. Some responses were hostile; others were not very encouraging. On 19 March 1987, the Shaftesbury Trust responded by sending their representative to inspect the premises. That visit, though quite amicable, did not yield the desired results as the Shaftsbury Trust was only interested in new buildings, and would have to own the Scheme.

In April, an official of the Housing Authority Charitable Trust visited and made helpful suggestions, but yet the solution was not found as their grants were not made for such purposes. The aid being sought was to repair and convert certain rooms of the Overstone building for a home for the elderly.

Following a meeting at which HRH Prince Charles challenged various societies to offer more aid to ethnic minority groups in the Inner Cities, Kaye Leverington, of the Abbeyfield Society, Potters Bar, visited Overstone on 25 June 1987. She had received one of Joyce's letters with a photograph of Overstone, but had not given it much consideration. However, at the nudging of His Royal Highness at that meeting, she had an impulse to pay a visit to Overstone. That day was the day of salvation. Kaye made a thorough inspection of the building and wrote back to say that, in all likelihood, a Senior Citizens home could be established there. However, it was necessary for a Trust to be formed to undertake the establishment and running of the home.

The National Executive Committee of the NTCG examined the idea of leasing the East Wing of the Main House for the development of an Elderly Home, and its implications to the overall functioning of the other activities on the premises. It was felt that there was sufficient room to accommodate the venture and the programme was given approval.

On Saturday 19 September, 1987 the Vice-Chairman of the Abbeyfield Society accompanied by the Regional Secretary and Kaye Leverington, the Director of Projects, visited Overstone at a meeting of the Ministers, Women's Presidents and Site Team. He announced the acceptance of the local group that was formed and named Abbeyfield Dorcas Afro-Carib Society. The group was advised to seek registration as a Housing Association, after affiliation with Abbeyfield-Potters Bar, and a promise was made of a grant. The Society has since been registered by the Housing Corporation. From that time, the Church began raising funds to assist in the programme, and it was anticipated that with grant aid, eleven bed-sits for the lonely elderly, and a flat for a resident warden would be provided. That was easier said than done. The struggles and set-backs to this ideal are too many to be mentioned in this brief report. But suffice it to say, now four years down the road, the struggle is still on. Some of the leaders of the Dorcas committee gave up and resigned; some confessed their frustration at the bureaucratic nightmare into which they were thrown. But Joyce, the Administrator, seemed to cry out like Jacob when he wrestled with the angel, 'I will not let you go, unless you bless me!' (Gen. 32.26). It was on that blessed day when Terry Waite was released that news was received that the Housing Corporation had finally commissioned the Scheme, and operations were shortly to begin. The present Committee consisting of Dr. C. L. Ryan (Chairman), Winston Willis (former Chairman in the heat of the struggle), V. Brown, Secretary, L. Miller (former Secretary), R. Scott, Treasurer, S. Curtis, Dr S. Lawrence, G. Smart and J. Alexander anxiously longed for the start up of the project for which they had struggled so long. They have all confessed that had it not been for the tenacity and persistence of Joyce, who has been the driving force, they would have long written it off as a hopeless exercise. For Joyce, this has been her dream, night and day—an unrelenting burden—to see better housing for Black Elderly who have laboured hard in this country, and now need adequate care in an environment that is not too far removed from their roots. The Dorcas committee are no doubt gratified to see the commencement of their dream. The support of the Church in prayer, giving and encouragement has stood them in good stead. The conversion work began on December 9, 1991.

It is also worthy of note, that another house that was acquired by Dorcas at Streatham, London for the Lonely Elderly, is also being rehabilitated to provide seven bed-sits and one House-keeper's flat. Both projects should be completed within the next year. It is the intention of the Dorcas Society to develop more housing for the lonely Elderly, and homeless, regardless of colour or race, in needy areas throughout the country.

The completion of these two projects by the ending of 1992 will mark a significant development in the Church's move from scepticism of its role in these areas of social concern. The recent increase in homelessness across the nation makes the NTCG's task more urgent. Conditions are predicated to be precarious in the days ahead, and the Church must engage in serious planning and programming if it must meet its commitment to care.

7. Evaluation of Project

As we gathered around the table as a Site Team to evaluate the project there was a feeling of deep satisfaction that at last an attempt had been made to tackle and document some of the issues that have affected the Church over the years. But not only so, we were also thrilled to be able to see tangible evidences of the success of our efforts. Only two members of the group were absent; one due to illness, and the other due to uncontrollable circumstances.

The paper was read chapter by chapter with each member having an opportunity to comment. At the end of the exercise, it was noted that change goal 1 of the change goals was achieved, i.e., the setting up of the Department of Social Responsibility. And, the second change goal, i.e., to sensitize the African-Caribbean people to the benefits working in co-operation with each other, was bearing fruits. As we were meeting to evaluate the project, a number of our men drawn from around the country were also meeting at our Church at Highgate, Birmingham, to discuss the formation of a company. (This idea was highlighted at our National Laymen's seminar held 27-29 November 1987). Unfortunately, while some men have formed their own companies, owing to the present state of the economy, not many have been successful. However, one such venture that so far has made some headway is Sapphire, set up by a group of young people to handle video recordings of the churches' conventions and other activities. This has been a great boost to the Church in getting out its message.

Goal Achievement

(a) ADMINISTRATION GOAL 1

As far as the first Administrative Goal was concerned, the Department was set up and was functioning. The Director had presented his report on the feasibility study which was made on the project on Friday 29 January 1988. Several dignitaries from the community were present including the Mayor of Northampton and a representative of Barclays Bank that made the grant for the development worker.

The Director of the Department of Social Responsibility, Arnold Kirlew, also reported to the Site Team on visits he made to local Churches his observation of the developments of their projects. In his estimation there was growing appreciation at the grassroots for the direction the Church was now providing. It might be useful to state his reflections of his personal growth and what participation in the project meant to him. He noted:

The Site Team has provided a forum to assess and openly discuss the organization objectively. It has given me an opportunity to develop my understanding of the history of the NTCG, and the role my parents played in its development.

The fact that the Site Team consisted of people of different professional vocations, age groups, and positions within the organization, assisted me in broadening my knowledge of our faith and the way individuals interpret it, in the light of their occupation, age, experience, and position within the community. It also enabled me to develop my analytical skills, and provided an opportunity for cross-fertilization of ideas and experiences to take place. The issues addressed by the Site Team were relevant to the development and future of the NTCG in Britain.'

Speaking of his personal delight at the attempt to raise the political conscious-ness of the membership, the Director continued to express in strong emotions:

'For me, I felt it was the first time we, as a a Church had addressed the socio-economic and political issues with a view of doing something positive about them.

'The history of African Caribbeans in England is different to that of Blacks in the U.S.A. Notwithstanding, there are similarities in our struggle for liberation. The Black-led Churches in Britain, unlike the Black Churches in America, have remained silent. The results of this project will lead to means of rectifying this situation, not by launching any political campaign, but by providing a balanced programme of socio-economic activities, which will deliver the necessary care-based services for people who have worked tirelessly over the years to build the NTCG, and secondly, to the poor and destitute.

Referring to his personal growth and change of feelings towards the work of the Site Team, and his appreciation for being a part of the group, he continued:

'On reflection, my first feeling when I joined I joined the Site Team has changed from one of scepticism to one of hope, because a start has been made—problems have been identified. Confidence, because we now have a leadership committed to providing the necessary mechanism to bring about the realization that caring is practical and necessary. The project has opened my eyes to other areas of life and given me an insight and knowledge of the world that I would not have otherwise been able to attain.

'My honest evaluation of the project is simply this, it is feasible because there is a demand. It will fulfil the needs of an increasing population of people whom for years, have been left to rely on the insensitive nature of institutions which do not understand, or are unable to provide for their "real" needs.

'Previously, the British Church pioneered the development of social care via the Welfare State, and acted as a voice for the disadvantaged in the community. Today, the onus is placed on government to interpret the needs of the same groups and provide adequate services.

'This project will point the NTCG to regain the initiative and begin to re-enact a role that was once at the top of its agenda.'

With such an honest appraisal from the one appointed as Director of the Department, it was expected that the project would move forward rapidly and with much enthusiasm. It was felt that in his summation, he encapsulated the sentiments of all the members of the Site Team.

Following the launch of the Department of Social Responsibility, the Director visited several churches throughout the country. His main emphases were:

1. to identify the needs of local churches and residents of the communities served by them;
2. to motivate and raise consciousness and provide development guidelines by talking to the ministers and members;
3. explaining how to establish Community programmes.

Areas covered were London, Coventry, Derby, Nottingham, Bilston, Birmingham, and Stoke-on-Trent. Topics covered include:

How to draw up a Constitution
How to form a Committee
The methods of conducting meetings
The duties and responsibilities of appointed officers
Communicating with local Councils
Lobbying local Councillors to gain support and recognition
How to complete an application form for funding from local Councils
What is available and how to apply for it
Training voluntary workers
How to keep financial records
Accounting systems and controls
Project management and setting clear aims and objectives

The Director found that many Churches he visited were contemplating embarking on a social programme, but were in the main, discouraged because of the costs and lack of readily 'in house' expertise.

However, after meeting and outlining the nature and methods of establishing community care programmes, all the Churches were left with a clear idea of the sort of programmes they could establish within the restraints of the Churches' buildings, budget and expertise.

Most Churches, both North and South, began to realize that senior citizens' programmes and youth recreation and leisure activities were the projects best suited for their locality. As has been mentioned earlier, a fair percentage of the membership and users of the Church have reached and were nearing retirement age. Many senior citizens were unemployed and a good number suffering from ailments common to people originating from the African Caribbean countries, such as high-blood pressure, diabetes, rheumatoid arthritis, etc.

In most cases, the local Authorities were not making provisions for Black Elderly, and consequently, most Black Elderly spent their time at home wasting away. Many were ignorant of subsidies available to White, or in certain cases, elderly people from other ethnic groups due to the fact that there were not many established Black senior citizens clubs recognized by the Local Authorities, or other organizations, such as Age Concern or Help-the-Aged. A case in point was when free butter and meat were being distributed by Government four years ago. That was done only through recognized agencies.

Another fact that was not taken into account were the special needs of Black elderly people. many were told to join White-run Clubs which did not pay attention to the dietary needs and recreational interests of that group. They were to accept what was going and be content. It was obvious that such attitudes only increased the discomfort of Black Elderly and led to non-participation in the clubs. The result was further isolation.

Since the project had been running, the Director reported that some Churches were embarking on establishing senior citizens' programmes to include: one day a week luncheon club, arts and crafts workshops, counselling, discussions, games, pick-up and delivery service for housebound and advice on welfare, housing and health matters.

Over the last few years, Churches at Willesden, Lee, Holloway, Hammersmith and West Croydon; Dudley, Coventry, and Leicester have improved their facilities to provide care for the Elderly. Existing projects at Brixton, and Willesden, in London, Handsworth, Wolverhampton, Sheffield and Leeds are making rapid progress. At Leeds, a property has been acquired with enough land to erect a Unit providing homes for the Elderly.

A unique programme is being run by one of our pastors, the Rev. Gofna Shepherd, whose members provide a meal at the Church on Sundays for the Elderly, a good number of whom are White. At the Anglican Church hall where they worship on Sundays, the Elderly are collected from their homes and served a meal prepared and brought to the hall. I was present at one such gathering when agents from the Social Services in the Aylesbury area visited and made a small presentation to aid the work being carried on by the Church. It is now being sponsored by the Aylesbury Vale Council and Aged Concern.

One can now clearly see that there has been a general movement towards a more positive and practical approach to our faith. This entails making provision for today's needs and changing the economic position of some who were for over six years unemployed.

The voluntary contributions of members who hold offices in this Department are commendable, for without their input the project would otherwise have failed.

(b) ADMINISTRATIVE GOAL 2
Since 1987, the Church has been emphasizing the need for co- operative ventures. This has been done through convention themes and seminar subjects. As has been mentioned in an earlier chapter, the year's general theme was 'Covenant to Care,' while the Ladies Ministries Department emphasized 'Responsibility to Care.' It was generally recognized that one could not care without co-operation.

With regard to the setting up of a co-operative project, I have observed with a bit of dismay that there is still a great lack of confidence in people's ability to deliver. Back in 1988 some of the men had gathered at Highate with much enthusiasm to consider the formation of a company. At least 25 men were reported to have agreed to contribute at least £500 each and select a steering committee to proceed with the formation of some kind of co-operative venture. This seemed to have been an ambitious move, and, as far as could be ascertained, was the first time such positive steps were contemplated. However, it has gone beyond the stage of perceived possibility into decisive action. What was seen as a spiritually motivated initiative has fallen far short of the mark. This is a matter of deep concern. I am yet to understand why we have not been able to reach that level of co-operation that will deliver the goods and services that are needed for our community.

For my own part, I appointed a ministerial intern, Tom Miller, who graduated from our College that July, 1988, to monitor my sermons to determine what effect the project had on my own theological reflections. His observations were that on each occasion he had been with me to a major meeting, my concerns for the socially oppressed came through loudly and clearly. He recalled a meeting at the Manchester Cathedral, at a multi-cultural service where I was the speaker. In his view, I appealed for the Church's social responsibility to be more than theological rhetoric. He also reported that a sermon delivered at Lambert Road, Brixton, 30 August 1987, was a most striking appeal to the youth urging them to move forward socially, economically, politically and spiritually. In his own words, Tom recalls the occasion thus:

'This sermon addressed the young people to make them aware of the fact that they can take on almost any career and maintain their blessing as Daniel was so very careful to do. This call was for them to "put God first", not just in their spiritual lives, but also their social lives. Many of the young people expressed to me after the service that they were challenged and satisfied because here was someone who not only appealed to their spiritual lives but their social lives within a Godly context.'

Tom also reported a conversation he had with a student from Cambridge University who had been visiting the Church for the first time that day. According to Tom, the student remarked:

'I am impressed to see the mature level of the Pastor's sermon where the Church and secular fields are concerned. He seemed to be very up-to-date and very broad where the link between social and spiritual responsibility of his people are concerned.'

Tom is not alone in his opinion that my sermons have been different over that period. I must admit that I had been speaking out, but I was quite shocked when, after preaching at a local Church on New Years's Sunday, 3 January, 1988, the Secretary of the Church said to me, 'This one was not political.' I inquired of her whether my sermons had seemed to be political in the past and her response was positive. She felt that the last three she had heard me preach dealt much with socio-economic issues. 'But,' she added, 'it was good for people's eyes to be opened, and for them to become more conscious of governmental concerns and the ways they can accomplish things together.' She explained that some of the members were not too concerned about such things, and it was good for them to hear it coming from the top.'

The move has now begun. It would be left to the leadership of the NTCG to keep up the momentum. It was felt that in areas where the leadership had deep conviction concerning the social needs of the community, the new initiatives would flourish, but where leaders were unwilling to involve themselves, there will be no impact. It is certain, however, that from the new insights revealed through this project that the New Testament Church of God can never be the same again.

For far too long Black people have carried as a legacy the scars of slavery. The slave owners succeeded in creating barriers that prevented the bonding among the slaves and so reduced the opportunities for insurrection. The pattern of divide-and-conquer was successfully used to destroy the natural bond that existed between the Black community. As K. Stampp observed:

'The slaveholder needed the willing co-operation of some of his bondsmen to make his government work efficiently. Knowing that the majority could not be trusted, he tried to recruit a few who would be loyal to him and take his side against others. Usually, he found his allies among the domestics, skilled artisans, and foremen, all of whom he encouraged to feel superior to, and remain apart from, field-hands ... In this manner, some planters gained the assistance of chattels who identified themselves wholly with the master class.'[1]

This kind of behaviour has passed on from generation to generation, even to this day where Blacks are not sufficiently conscious they have been exploited in the same manner. The competitiveness among themselves and the anxiety to achieve have not allowed them to move up together. Too many are led to believe that success can only be achieved in isolation and fraternization outside their community. This bias must be eradicated and a sense of wholeness and soundness in co-operativeness needs to be embedded in the minds of the younger generation. It might be too late for the older generation, but there is hope for the younger generation; one that must use the abundant resources now available among them as a force for upward mobility. This generation must demand equal participation in the affairs of this country and seek not just what they can acquire for themselves, but what they can contribute to making the society a better one. The young British Blacks of African Caribbean descent must know and assert their rights in this land. They are not just here on a temporary basis as their parents might have felt. This is the land of their birth and they have to establish themselves and be a part of it. The NTCG must endeavour to assist them to establish themselves and contribute their share to building this nation.

Anything less than this will be a denial of its responsibility to the masses of youth that see the Church as their heritage. If their parents have done nothing else for them, they have given them a faith and investment in the Church.

---

[1] K. Stampp, *The Peculiar Institution: Slavery in the Ante-Bellum South*, (Vintage Books, New York, 1956), p.79 quoted by Na'im Akbar, *Chains and Images of Psychological Slavery*, (New Mind Productions, Jersey City, New York, 1984), p.24.

8. Conclusion

Ministry for me has always been a challenge and a great sense of fulfilment. In my thirty-five years experience, which took me from pastoring a small congregation in a ground-floor room of an East Indian family in Bossiere Village, Port of Spain, to National leadership in Britain, by way of mission fields in West Africa, I have always poured myself into every venture, recognizing the fact that it was a God appointed task.

This project was entered into with no less zeal, but I was to experience a measure of awakening that I had never anticipated. I began the journey quite sure of where I wanted to go. My own ambition was to see a great spiritual renewal within our denomination, through the revival of the hope in a brighter tomorrow. I felt that our Church needed to renew the commitment to the holy faith once delivered to our fathers,' and the only way to accomplish that was by redefining and emphasizing our own distinctives. This project was to assist me in identifying those areas of our spiritual decay and to motivate our evangelistic fervour in correcting them and so put the Church back on its spiritual course, in anticipation of the imminent return of our Blessed Lord and Saviour Jesus Christ.

Now that I have completed the project, I have been so enlightened and awakened that for me it has really just begun. It is hard to admit that after thirty years of preaching the hope of the Church, I had not, until within the last four years, wrestled with concepts that I promulgated, nor been so radically affected. I had never before questioned the idea that radical commitment to Christ meant anything other than a total denial of the self-life, in order to serve the Christ-life. Spiritual life for me meant a commitment to doing and being all that one can become in Christ to the total subjugation of the material life. That side did not matter in this life; all that I understood that mattered was one's spiritual relationship with Christ and the Father. I believed that God met one's need according to his riches in glory by Christ Jesus' (Phil. 4.19); one was then to divorce oneself completely from all mundane consequentials so as to gain '. . . the prize of the high calling of God in Christ Jesus' (Phil. 3.14). I still hold these concepts dear, but in a different dimension. I have had to question them in the light of the suffering of God's people, his promise of hope in this life, and the life to come.

I believe the Kingdom has been advanced in that I can now better conceptualize the hope that has meaning in the here and now and not one that was only pertinent to the 'by and by.' I have always taken to task those who have regarded my hope as merely pie in the sky.' I still do, for I believe that there is something to hope for in the 'tomorrow'. But what I have learnt is that tomorrow' has begun today.

Another area in which this project has affected the Site Team and me is in the area of Black-consciousness. Perhaps it has affected me more than it affected them. Some were very Black-conscious, having grown up in the Inner City and been exposed to the effects of social rejection due to one's colour. For me, it was different. I came to this country as an adult, and really could not point to any one instance where my colour came into question. I had also been out of the country ministering among people of my own colour (though not of the same culture) for a considerable number of years. It was, therefore, a struggle for me to understand all the fuss about 'Black Theology', 'White Theology', and terms like Black Consciousness' and even 'Racism.' But of these were the issues that the Church was wrestling with at the grassroots. From my vantage point, however, these were irrelevant to the meaning of the gospel. It had not dawned on me over the years that I had not come to grips with 'who I am.'

I think the best way to explain it is perhaps the unique way in which the Ghanaians described me when I served as a missionary in Ghana. I was always referred to as 'Bibini broni', which literally meant, Black White-man'. To some large extent that was unconsciously true of me. Deep within was a denial of my negritude. When I was a boy, I can recall that one of the ways by which we ridiculed each other was to imply that one was 'black.' I therefore grew up not to see myself as 'Black' or having any Black values. I knew I was not 'White.' Perhaps I had no colour, for certainly I was not 'Black.'

The obvious conscious stance then was that colour did not matter in the Kingdom of God. Since there was no conscious confrontation with this fact, I could not fully empathize with those who had suffered the raw brutality of racial hatred and brazen discrimination because of their colour.

This study has awakened in me a consciousness of who I am. It has not produced a negative effect, but a positive one.

Having lived and worked in Africa, I can appreciate the values and rich heritage of my forebears. And, whereas I had in the past refused to come to grips with my true person, I can now feel a sense of pride of being who I am. Through this project I have learnt in a more meaningful way that:

'I was made in his likeness,
Created in his image;
For I was born to serve the Lord.
And I know I can't deny him,
I'll always walk beside him,
For I was born to serve the Lord.' *(Unknown).*

(b) PROJECT FUTURE

The project has a future. It will be continued because there are lots of areas that have not been researched and uncovered. The idea is highly relevant because of the growing assertiveness of British Black youths, the enlightenment among the older generation in the face of growing racism, and hardening attitudes in the wider society due to economic pressures. This militancy need not lead to the abandonment of law and order, but must be harnessed and channelled for the better progress of society and the Kingdom of God. Just as any river could over-flow its banks at flood time and wreak havoc and destruction, so can uncontrolled zeal without proper knowledge wreak havoc in any community determined to seek its human rights. To quote Lord Scarman's advice to minorities at the Black Rights (UK) and the Commission for Racial Equality Conference held 19 November 1988:

'They must not withdraw from the mainstream of British society however alienated some may understandably feel at present under the pressure of current frustrations and deprivations. They must use to the full the educational and training facilities offered. If they cannot achieve power, and many of us never will, they can by example and industry exert influence. They must accept the logic of their settlement in this country by recognizing themselves as truly British people and co-heirs with the majority to the British tradition and culture. This they can do while retaining pride in their origins and in the history and customs of their people. They must work for, as well as in, Britain, the country of their settlement—and increasingly the country of their birth.

'It is the nation's duty to open them the door of opportunity but they must make the effort to walk through it, seize the opportunities to which the door must be seen to give access.'[1]

This is indeed very sound and veritable advice and the Church would do well to encourage its constituency to take note. Black resilience in the Black-led Churches should be harnessed to restore better racial harmony within the community and a better quality of life for the future.

Because of the time it took the Site Team and me to come to understand the nature of the problem, we have only just begun the research. Our commitment must be a continuing process of:

(a) Identifying the social and economic needs of the members of the NTCG.

(b) Formulating policies relevant to these needs.

(c) Researching and collating statistical information on the resources and personnel within the organization

(d) Planning capital programmes that will generate necessary funds for social responsibility projects outside the funding of Government and other agencies.

(e) Providing a proper co-ordinating mechanism to bring together the expertise within the NTCG for the total benefit of the organization

I can see the future ministry of this Church as coming out of the shadows into the path where it can shed light to the thousands needing guidance. The NTCG cannot turn its back on the revealed needs within its constituency and the wider community. There must be greater participation in the affairs of the nation as the eyes of many have been opened.

---

[1] Keynote address by Lord Scarman quoted in *A conference report on the role of Black People, Human Rights and the Media*. Published by Black Rights (UK) (Rainbow Publishing Ltd., London, 1989), pp.31, 32.

The late Reverend Vernon Nelson, then pastor of the New Testament Church of God at Lambert Road, Brixton, as a result of the Church's new stance was encouraged to participate in *Everyman*, a programme on BBC 1 which was broadcast 13 December 1987. Many favourable responses were received from the viewers. To quote one of these:

'I am writing this note to thank you and your congregation for the wonderful message of hope which came across, to me and I feel sure to many others, in the *Everyman* programme last night. So often all we hear from the media is doom and gloom about the racial situation in this country, you really made me feel that the Lord is at work and one day we will all be able to live together as one body of God's people.

'I have no idea of how, or if, the Lord wants me to be of help in making this prayer a reality, but if you feel there is any way that we might help each other build bridges of friendship between your people ... I would be glad to follow this note with some action.' (D.R.)

Another viewer, commending the pastor for his performance while expressing his appreciation for the programme, wrote in part:

'... My highest commendation goes to Pastor Vernon Nelson for his sincerity, his courage to identify and speak out against the "festering sores" within our society, particularly in Education and the Church. I hope that he may feel inspired to spread his message because all our Inner Cities could benefit from his guidance.' (A.G.)

It must be noted that Brixton experienced two terrible riots, in 1981 and 1985, and, more recently, this year (1991) had its tensions which could have led to another. Since the riot of 1985, the local church at Brixton was a venue for the Police and Clergy to meet with members of the community to discuss ways to deal with the problems of that Inner City. The Church will endeavour, in the light of reports, to make clear to the Police its stance on Law and Order. And, at the same time, the Church will not be silent in bringing to the attention of those in authority, the abuse of power by some policemen who take advantage of the uniform to unleash their prejudices on innocent Black people. The reports of members who have been accosted and manhandled for no reason other than that they were perceived to be of the wrong colour and in the wrong place are alarming. The Church must not, however, be deterred by these reports in its efforts to present the right image and respect for the Police. The following letter from the Chief Superintendent of Police, Brixton, to the local pastor is evidence of what was being done, and the type of relationship the NTCG would encourage in the communities it serves. The Superintendent wrote:

'Dear Vernon:

I have delayed writing in order to get some reaction to our recent Gospel Concert.

Now it is time to sincerely thank you, your choirs and the members of your congregation who so strongly supported us on that evening.

It was a pleasure for me to experience again the joy of your Church worship. It really is an inspiration and you must feel proud of the younger members.

I was pleased too that other police officers and their wives were able to hear you speak and understand the way you wish the Church to give guidance and example to the young. The recent *Everyman* programme portrayed our community, your Church and your ideas in a calm and fair manner. I am quite sure many people will have been encouraged by what they saw and who knows what seed may have been sown?

For my part, I hope 1988 brings even closer co-operation between the Churches and the Police. I think in that way we will learn from one another about the matters that trouble people most and about how we can tackle those problems in the most successful way.

On behalf of everyone at Brixton Police Station thank you to all for your enduring effort, and warmest good wishes for the New Year.

Sincerely,' (RM)

Such a heart-warming letter expresses the need and the possibilities for right relationship to exist between Blacks and the Police. The Church and the Police are working to maintain order in the society. The Police from the angle of the Law, while the Church can be said to approach it from grace. Since the laws of the land are built on Judeo-Christian principles which the Church seeks to uphold, there is no reason why the objectives of maintaining law and order could not be achieved. In principle it could be said the Church is in tandem with the Police in terms of justice and obedience to the law. But is this an ideal too unrealistic to entertain, given the bitter experience of unreasonable harassment people suffer at the hand of some unscrupulous officers?

The project has awakened many, and will in future realize many more valuable spin-offs. For instance, since the project, members have felt more comfortable to take part in social activities than they did before. In the past they would have been looked upon as stepping out of line into areas of worldly concerns. But now, some ministers have seized opportunities to serve on Public Boards. Over the past two years, Eric Brown has served on the National Parole Board, and as a part-time Commissioner of the Commission for Racial Equality. Interestingly enough, he was a member of the Site Team. Others have accepted positions as Prison Chaplains, Lay-visitors and Chaplain to the Police. It is evident that more leaders will seek opportunity to make their full contribution to serve the community without former reservations.

(c) THEOLOGY

It was observed that the New Testament Church of God was faced with the dilemma of maintaining a hope in the imminent return of Christ, and yet be concerned about the spiritual implications of the liberating effect of the gospel. It is tempting for some just to divest themselves of all material concerns and wait for the Lord to come. That might have been the cause of the actions of the early Church as recorded in Acts 4. Many of the wealthy members sold all they had and brought the money to the apostles to be divided among those who had none. This, perhaps, was the first attempt at communism. But it also bred greed and unfaithfulness which resulted in the death of two members (Acts 5.1-11). It was in all probability, also, that which led to more poverty among the Church members at Jerusalem. Paul at one time had to solicit donations from the Gentile Church for them (1 Cor. 16.23). An over-emphasized eschatological hope of the literal return of Christ has through the history of the Christian Church led to the formation of various Apocalyptic movements. Members have been led to sell up all their possessions and wait for the day of the Lord to come.

I would suggest that some of the responses to such speculation could be found in the admonition of Christ to 'Occupy till I come' (Luke 19.13), and the parable of the talents in Matthew 25.14-30. There are other Scriptures, but these two speak very clearly to the issues at hand. In each instance the King or nobleman expected his servants to utilize their skills and improve their positions in anticipation of promotion when he should return. There is no suggestion, or idle speculation, that his return should be the beginning of their heritage.

The NTCG must encourage its members to toil until the final coming day of the Lord when he shall subdue all things; for, until such time, Christ is at work building his Kingdom. This Kingdom has come, but not yet in its fulness. There are some today who have a triumphalist belief or make-belief as to the fact that all things are now fully under his feet. But Scripture declares that '... he must reign till he has put all enemies under his feet' (1 Cor. 15.25). That day is not yet, but the light of that day has dawned upon us. For Black people in particular, this message must be made explicit. The day of emancipation has come. Christ the emancipator has broken the degrading and dehumanizing chains of slavery.

When I was a child, my parents kept chickens. Whenever a new addition was made to the number, it had to be tied with a cord to some post in the yard in order that it might get accustomed to its new owners. I used to notice that, after the chicken had been tied for several days, when it was loosed, it remained standing around the post. It was unconscious of the fact that it had been loosed. It had grown so accustomed to being bound and fed at the same place for so long that it would not leave even though it was now free.

That has been the case of the African Caribbeans today. Their forebears had been chained for so long and fed at the end of the master's rope that, psychologically, they have not yet understood what it is to be free. Even some Christians see their freedom possible only at the end of life's journey. The theology expressed in many songs still speaks of freedom yet to be realized. One of many examples is a 'Spiritual' song I have often heard sung with gusto, is an unconscious expression of the bondage symptomatic of African Caribbean people.

'Now when this life is over, and my work here is done,
When I've gone the last mile and the battle has been won;
I'm going to my home that is somewhere beyond the sky,
And there my Jesus he will be waiting up there on high.

There'll be singing and praising the Lord,
That's when we get our reward.
O' what a time we are going to find,
And we won't have to cry no more.

Chorus Soon will be done with this world,
      Soon will be done with this world;
      We won't have to cry no more.' (*Unknown*)

The writer could be expressing hope in tomorrow after the end of the mundane trials that befall all of God's children, and the promise that he will dry all our tears at the last day. But it also suggests that the writer, filled with despair, can find no hope but in the thought that death will bring comfort to all of life's sorrows. It should not be discredited that there is a hope in tomorrow, but it must also be emphasized that in Christ, here and now, the process has already begun. Indeed, we are more than conquerors through Christ. The whole truth is that African Caribbean people need to assert their freedom in Christ here and now. Slaves under bondage years ago could see no hope for a better tomorrow because of the endless torture and pain inflicted by their masters. For them to take comfort in such a song in their moments of utter helplessness and despair was understandable. For some, there was no hope for a better situation in this life, and they therefore had to succumb to their fate.

This might be the case of some Christians today; it should not be the norm for all. By this I mean, one may be crippled, blind and physically maimed and have to endure such conditions in anticipation that their suffering will end when life is over. That is in order; but for Christians to be subjugated, and in some cases, regarded as second-class citizens in the household of faith, and be encouraged to sing such a song, is a denial of the true realities of the Gospel. Like the man with the one talent in Matthew's account of the parable, who, instead of investing his talent, hid it. Even so some Black people have hidden from them the fact of freedom, and are awaiting deliverance only at the last day. They must be made to rejoice in the knowledge that Christ, in his victory over sin, death and the grave, has already won their deliverance. They need to take the risk and invest their hope in the fulfilment of God's promises here and now. Whenever and wherever this is done, they will experience abundant life (John 10.9-10). One the other hand, fear, distrust, and despair are the results of burying their talents and reposing in a deliverance only at the end of life's journey. Why languish in scepticism? Hope in today.

(d) MISSIONS AND MINISTRY

A week before Christmas 1987, I attended a conference for Church leaders held at Cobham. Among other challenging presentations was a visual on the Changing Trends in Britain today. It was revealed that Britain had more preachers than doctors. That arrested my attention, especially in the light of the apparent feeble response to the appeal of the gospel. My mind has been continually plagued by the question, what is wrong with our mission and ministry to today's society?

In the theological reflections during the project, we identified our failure was our neglect in presenting the gospel as a hope to be experienced in the here and now. It was felt that enough emphasis was not placed on the fact that salvation was a living reality for the total person, not just the spiritual side only.

It is hoped that in this work those who need assurance that Christ's sacrificial death brought full deliverance, and offers a fulness of life now, may discover this reality.

The Seventies and Eighties have been years in Britain when people seemed to have lost hope in the established denominations. The debate over the Archbishop's comment on some of the causes for the senseless behaviour of youths on estates in some of our cities is an example of society's readiness to take on Church Leaders. This should not deter the Church from addressing the issues, and be a Voice for God. Poverty and social deprivation breed contempt. The have-nots seek to draw attention to their plight as they watch the growing affluence of the jet-setters as they race into the twenty-first century. They are demanding a right to a good time in their own ways which are, however, lawless, immoral and unacceptable. No one should support their behaviour; but none can deny that there are social factors that are linked to them.

On the other hand, there are those young people who have come to realize that permissiveness is not the answer to their search for true reality. They are looking for something more meaningful in life. The mission of the Church is to provide the answer for those youths.

Not too long ago, a gang leader who was confronted with the gospel by his brother found that he could not get over the uncanny feeling that came over him. Later, when one of his rivals attempted to slash him, he did not retaliate and he could not understand why. He later went to the Lee Church where the pastor led him to surrender his life to Christ. This experience led to a change in his personality and conduct. In time, he publicly confessed how knowing Christ had delivered him from his drug habits and witchcraft. Later, as he was being baptized, his mother who did not usually attend church came to witness her son's baptism. She too surrendered to the Lord and has since been baptized. Not only so, other members of his gang have been converted. His older brother who was sceptical of his professed change has also since followed him to the Church. Now there is a whole family finding satisfaction in serving God and living a decent life in society. The streets are safer because 'Mad Alf' as he was called has been changed by Christ. This is the mission the NTCG will continue to pursue.

Everyday, up and down this country, people are finding that in the Christ whom we preach, there is hope from scepticism. Wherever humankind falls in submission to Christ's control and recognizes him as Lord there is Hope.

Living in Christ does not warrant a dichotomy between one's spiritual and secular pursuits; rather, Christ must impact upon daily life and all its activities. The words of Paul are so relevant here, when he intoned:

> 'I am crucified with Christ, nevertheless, I live; yet not I, but Christ lives in me; and *the life I now live in the flesh* I live by faith in the Son of God who loved me, and gave himself for me' (Gal. 2.20 *mine*)

The Department of Social Responsibility would seek to correct this division between the secular and the sacred, and to guide the Church into a ministry in which Christ is central and the needs of humanity are his concern.

The goals which this project has attempted to establish are therefore, both timely and urgent. What has been achieved can be repeated, refined, and expanded as a programme guide for mission and ministry in the ensuing years. The message disseminated through the Churches, will serve as a catalyst for the ministry and mission of the NTCG. Away with scepticism; Christ is our Hope for today.

Appendix 1

NEW TESTAMENT CHURCH OF GOD

NAME OF COUNTY	TOWN/CITY
AVON	Bath Bristol
BEDFORDSHIRE	Luton
BERKSHIRE	Reading Slough
BUCKINGHAMSHIRE	Aylesbury High Wycombe Milton Keynes
CAMBRIDGESHIRE	Cambridge Huntingdon Peterborough
CHESHIRE	Crewe
DERBYSHIRE	Chesterfield Derby Long Eaton
GLOUCESTERSHIRE	Gloucester
GREATER LONDON	Balham Brixton Charlton Clapham Clapton Deptford Ealing Elephant & Castle E. Dulwich East Ham Edmonton Enfield Harrow Hammersmith Hendon Holloway Herne Hill Ilford Mile End Romford Vauxhall W. Croydon Willesden Woodgreen
GREATER MANCHESTER	Bolton Manchester (Chorlton) Cheetham Hill Longsight Oldham
HAMPSHIRE	Aldershot Basingstoke Southampton
HEREFORD/WORCESTER	Redditch
HERTFORDSHIRE	Hitchin Stevenage St Albans
KENT	Rochester
LEICESTERSHIRE	Leicester
NORTHAMPTONSHIRE	Northampton Wellingborough
NOTTINGHAMSHIRE	Nottingham Worksop
OXFORDSHIRE	Oxford
SALOP	Wellington
SOUTH YORKSHIRE	Sheffield Firvale
STAFFORDSHIRE	Burton-on-Trent Stafford Stoke-on-Trent
WARWICKSHIRE	Nuneaton Rugby
WEST MIDLANDS	Birmingham Brookfield Castle Vale Erdington Handsworth Highgate Kingshurst Bilston Coventry Walsall Wednesfield Willenhall Wolverhampton
WEST YORKSHIRE	Bradford Halifax Huddersfield Leeds
WILTSHIRE	Chippenham Trowbridge
WALES	Cardiff Newport

Churches are grouped under districts and supervised by a District Overseer

DISTRICT	SUPERVISOR
ALDERSHOT	B.O. Burrell
BILSTON	L. Bailey
BRISTOL	K. G. Walder
BRIXTON	C. E. Fisher
COVENTRY	A. J. Walters
DEPTFORD	H. Strachan
DERBY	K. Channer
DUDLEY	L. A. Jackson
GLOUCESTER	C. Scott
HANDSWORTH	S. U.Thompson
HIGHGATE	P. Williams
LEE	U. L. Simpson
LEEDS	C. L. Hastings
LEICESTER	F. Mitchell
LUTON	H. Gayle
MANCHESTER	T. E. Caine
READING	I. Lawrence
SHEFFIELD	B. Grey
STOKE-ON-TRENT	E. Johns
WEST CROYDON	W. C. Willins
WILLESDEN	I. Lewinson
WOLVERHAMPTON	W. L. Willis
WOOD GREEN	E. Brown

The highest national governing Body is the National Executive Council, with the National Overseer as Executive Chairman. The present Executive Council is comprised of the following: S. E. Arnold (National Overseer), R. H. Parkinson (National Secretary). Members: I. Lewinson, E. Brown, C. E. Fisher, C. L. Hastings, L. A. Bailey, Willis, H. Gayle, S. U. Thompson, I. Lawrence, J. Edwards. Members of the Council may hold office for up to six consecutive years but must stand for re-election every two years. The following lead the Auxiliary Movements within the Church.

National Evangelist .... I. Newland
Youth and Christian Education ...... D. Webley
Director of Ladies Ministries .... M. J. Arnold
Director of Laymen Ministries .... J. Grey
Social Responsibility .... W. Williams
National Accountant .... W. Morgan
Deed of Covenant Administrator .... J. Hall

Theological education began at a Bible Institute at George Street, Lozells, Birmingham, in 1963. The Church now operates a residential college at Overstone, and two extension schools at Birmingham and London.

C. L. Ryan .... Principal of Overstone College
L. George .... Principal Ebenezer Bible Institute, Birmingham
G. Andrews .... Administrator, E.B.I. London

Appendix 2

1964 The General Election, P. Griffiths became Conservative M.P. for Smethwick, Birmingham, against the national 'swing' to Labour, with a racist campaign using the slogan 'If you want a nigger neighbour, vote Labour.' Harold Wilson asked that he be treated as 'a parliamentary leper'

From

1967 The National Front has been advocating 'Keep Britain White'

1968- Enoch Powell made a series of inflammatory, self-fulfilling prophecies
1970 and was expelled from the Conservative Party

1978 Mrs. Thatcher spoke of 'cultural swamping' in a television interview as a prelude to the 1979 Election which the Conservatives won

1983 'Race' was hardly raised as an issue during the election but the Conservative victory may indicate electoral approval for their hard line on immigration and nationality etc.

Delegates at the Conservative Party Conference, Autumn 1983, voted to consider a motion on 'voluntary repatriation', although it was heavily defeated

Bi-partisan policy on 'race' and 'immigration'

A bi-partisan policy (Labour and Conservative) has developed during the period since the war, based upon the argument that if numbers of 'immigrants' (meaning black immigrants) are restricted, better will be the opportunities for all and the greater chances of internal peace. This has been almost constantly demonstrated as a fallacy, not least by the 'riots' of 1981, and the rapid increase in unemployment.

Party	Immigration	Race Relation	Party	Buffering' Institutions
CON	Commonwealth Immigration Act 1962	Race Relations Act 1965	LAB	Race Relations Board
LAB	Commonwealth Immigration Act 1968	Race Relations Act 1968	LAB	Community Relations Council
CON	Immigration Act 1971	Race Relations Act 1976	LAB	Commission for Racial Equality

This bi-partisan policy has effectively:

—halted immigration of people from the New Commonwealth, so affecting the reunion of families and the right of black people to enter Britain.

—created an extra-judicial control upon immigrants with use of custodial measures as for criminals;

—constructed the 'buffering' machinery of the Commission for Racial equality and its local branches, which has not helped black citizens enter normal political activity;

—defined the 'British' and those who can exercise democratic rights in Britain.

Conflict in the Cities

Southall, 1976 and 1979, St Paul's Bristol 1980 and 1983, Brixton, Toxteth etc, 1981. (Brixton, Handsworth, 1985 can be added).
The official responses have been:
—an enquiry by Lord Scarman—*The Brixton Disorder;*
—an initiative on Merseyside, headed by Michael Hastings;
—an increase in the establishment of the Metropolitan Police;
—a new Police and Criminal Evidence Bill.

It is important to take account of the varying explanations for the disturbances;

From a White establishment point of view
—youthful exuberance and frustration at the lack of facilities in the Inner Cities;
—criminal activity (drug peddling etc) which the police were attempting to counter but the criminals reacted to protect themselves;
—outside' political interference, whether of the 'right'
or
—the 'left,' which disturbed the usually peaceful situation;
—'racism,' although this factor has usually been discounted.

From a black point of view
—disturbances were 'uprisings' against 'Babylon', a rejection of Western materialism, competitive individualism and institutionalized racism;
—uprisings (in which white youths joined with black youths in Brixton, Toxteth) justified by marginalization of the inner city neighbourhoods, use of police harassment, etc.

Population trends: Net emigration has exceeded immigration since 1945 yet Britain is still believed to be an over-crowded island. White people remain in positions of power and authority, for example, as doctors, social workers, teachers, police, politicians, employers, etc., in areas where most of them do not live.

Cycle of Deprivation: Black people have often become trapped within a cycle of deprivation in inner city neighbourhoods. more so than their white counterparts. The cumulative effect of racial disadvantage (for example, in housing, employment, education etc).

This information taken from Sue Colan & Maurice Hobbs, *New Humanity,* (BRCJ, Birmingham, 1984).

For Further Information
G. K. Lewis , *Slavery, Imperialism and Freedom* (Monthly Review Press, 1978);
Peter Fryer, *Staying Power: History of Black people in Britain* (Pluto Press, 1984)

Appendix 3

DEVELOPMENT CYCLE
STAGE A
Phase 1a. Conversion of a section of Overstone into a National Conference Centre.
Phase 1b. Establish accommodation for the Elderly in East Wing
Phase 1c. National computer training centre
Phase 2 Launch the National Community Action Programme
Phase 3 Partnership with the DOE or DTI to utilize part of 33½ acres of land into African Caribbean farm, producing African Caribbean and Asian agricultural products (e.g. sweet potatoes, mints, cerosee etc).

Sources of Funds
Phase 1a. Department of Environment
Phase 1b. Department of Environment
Local Council Section 8 Residential Homes Act 1980
Fundraising Programme
Phase 1c. European Economic Community
Department of Employment
Phase 2 Home Office (Staff and Voluntary expense)
Local Authorities;
Department of Health and Social Security
Voluntary Projects Programme
Sheltered employment and training for the disabled.
Phase 3 Department of Trade and Industry
European Economic Community
Trusts and Charities
The Countryside Commission
The Development Commission

Other sources of funding include:
a) Sports Council
b) The Commission for Racial Equality
c) The Equal Opportunities Commission

Immediate Requirements
Staffing: National Director, Finance Co-ordinator, Administrator.
Job Description Post: NATIONAL DIRECTOR
Purpose of Job
1. To be responsible for the co-ordination and development of the Community Action Programme.
2. To devise and implement strategies for fund-raising, recruitment, administration.

3. To design and initiate the national network to include already established project under the umbrella of the NTCG and to incorporate new development initiatives in the areas of Enterprise, Education, Social Welfare, Arts, Technology and Recreation.
4. To responsible for the provision and co-ordination of the following departments: finance, training, personnel, administration, legal, community relations and enterprise service.
5. To ensure good liaison between the Department of Social Responsibility and other departments of the NTCG, external agencies and the community.

Responsible to: The National Overseer or Chief Executive
Responsible for: Assistant Director, Finance Coordinator, Administrator, Regional Directors and District Managers.

Duties
1. To ensure that all activities of the department are kept within the constitution of the NTCG
2. To propose and implement a corporate plan for the development of the Department of Social Responsibility and to oversee its implementation and review.
3. To advise the Executive Committee on priority areas of work for the future development and management of the programme.
4. To ensure that the department's capital and revenue expenditure is kept within the budget.
5. To keep the overall staffing structure under review.
6. To devise work programmes and priorities for each region in co-operation with the Regional Directors and to ensure these programmes are implemented.
7. To co-ordinate all grant applications to statutory funding agencies. To act as main point of liaison between the Department and these agencies and to ensure that grant conditions are met by all regions.
8. To ensure that the Finance Co-ordinator maintains satisfactory financial accounting systems and provides monthly statements on the Department's financial position.
9. To arrange for advice and assistance as appropriate to assist in the development of the Department of Social Responsibility.
10. To provide training for Directors and Managers as required.
11. To be directly responsible for the development of co-operatives, small businesses, national schemes and other initiatives determined to be of benefit to the Organization (NTCG).

Job Description Post: FINANCE CO-ORDINATOR
Purpose of Job
1. To devise and implement an accounting system for the national Community Action Programme.
2. To advise the National, Regional and District Directors on projected income and expenditure

Responsible to: National Overseer & National Director
Responsible for: The Accounts Department

Duties:
1. To work with the National and Regional Directors in order to design and implement a national accounting system.
2. To provide support and assistance for Regional Directors on all matters relating to finance.
3. To ensure that all books are maintained and monthly reports are made available.
4. To provide quarterly finance reports for external funding agencies.
5. To assist the National Director with the department' fund raising programme.
6. To provide training for Junior staff as required.
7. To ensure that all necessary documents are processed to the relevant government departments.
8. To ensure that the P.A.Y.E. system is maintained.
9. To set up budgetary control and monitoring systems for each region with the respective Directors.
10. To advise the National Director on matters relating to improving the department's financial position.
11. To ensure that books are prepared for annual audit.

Job Description Post: ADMINISTRATOR
Purpose of Job
1. To set up and maintain an administrative system to include the processing of all grant applications, sorting of mail and correspondence to external agencies.
2. To set up office procedure and control and to ensure that all Junior staff within the offices are trained in order to process, store and interpret incoming and outgoing correspondence

Duties
1. To set up an office system procedure which will cope with the incoming/outgoing correspondence of the office.
2. To co-ordinate monthly reports from the Regional Directors.
3. To take minutes at National meetings and ensure that written agencies are prepared and circulated well in advance of meetings.
4. To be the main point of contact and to advise Regional and District Managers on the appropriate time-table for submitting information to the National office and other government departments.
5. To train Junior staff as necessary.
6. To ensure that sufficient stationary is purchased.
7. To be responsible for the processing of invoices and personal correspondence to external agencies.
8. To undertake other duties which may be required by the National Director.

Job Description Post: DISTRICT MANAGER
Purpose of Job

To be responsible for the workforce and their coodination, in order to ensure that all programmes and activities are carried out efficiently.

Responsible to: Regional Director

Duties:

1. To work with the Regional Director and advise him/her on matters relating to the development and progress of his/her district.
2. To train, motivate and ensure that all staff carry out their duties effectively.
3. To be responsible for all items of equipment, stock and materials, and to ensure that they are kept in good working order.
4. To ensure that staffing levels are kept up to the required standard.
5. To provide training for all members of staff especially voluntary workers.
6. To make recommendations to the Regional Director on matters relating to development and progress of his/her district.
7. To be responsible for maintaining satisfactory budgetary controls and accounting systems.
8. To submit monthly reports to the Regional Director
9. To undertake other duties that may be required by the Regional Director.

Job Description Post: REGIONAL DIRECTOR
Purpose of Job

1. To be responsible for implementation of a balanced programme of activities and to ensure that expenditure is kept within the designated budget.
2. To recruit and train staff in order to ensure that the services provided are of the highest possible standard.
3. To co-ordinate local and fund raising strategies and maintain a close liaison with the Regional Council and other agencies,

Responsible to: National Director

Responsible for: District Managers, workers and voluntary staff.

Duties:

1. To implement and co-ordinate the recruitment of all staff and to advise the National Director on all matters relating to the development of his region.
2. To work with District Managers in order to ensure that each programme and service is of the highest standard.
3. To provide monthly reports to the National Office.
4. To ensure that managers, workers and voluntary staff are motivated and adequate training courses are available to assist them in their personal development.
5. To implement policy decision of the National Executive as related to him through the National Director.
6. To assist in the job placement of workers who have completed training.

Appendix 4

Questionnaire of interview with Mr Abdul Majid of the Asian Community held on 2 December 1987.

1. I understand that you are a community leader in this area of Birmingham. Could you briefly explain the nature of your involvement in the Asian Community?
2. What kind of projects are you operating?
3. How are you able to rally the support of your people?
4. What unifying effect has your religion on the work with the community?
5. How do you account for the co-operative nature of your people?
6. What co-operative action have you undertaken in the areas of employment, housing and education for your community?
7. How responsive or negative have you found the indigenous society?
8. In what ways do you feel the Asian and Black communities can co-operate more fully in making a positive contribution to the community?
9. How long have you been working in this area, and what co-operative developments do you anticipate for the future?

Appendix 5

In April 1986 a group of people from the Caribbean community met with a view to creating a co-operative where the wealth of the community could be positively developed through full participation of members.

The basic principle of the idea was drawn up by Mr Thomas, a leading member of the Church and who has been an activist within the community. The idea was that members of the community contribute a minimum of £10.00 to a central collecting unit where elected Directors were charged with the responsibility of investing the money, in the first instance, into a business and/or funds as appropriate.

The benefit to the community would be realized when you use the Co-operative's services provided by the central body. To put it in a nutshell, you benefit from the profits of the Co-operative only when you purchase or use the service created by the central body.

From the meeting on 29 April 1986, a steering committee was set up and given the responsibility to go away and formulate the Co-operative Enterprise. We reported back to the general group on 29 September 1986 with our proposed policy for the Co-operative. After a time of discussion and ratification, the policy was agreed.

From this meeting, twelve Directors were appointed. Those who served on the steering committee plus another four from the general group were appointed. The twelve Directors were also known as the founder members.

As founder members of the C.C.E., this group felt the need to inform the wider community of its findings for the function of the Co-operative Enterprise.

The main areas of the policy statement were as follows:

The general constitution is contained in the General Rules for an industrial and provident Society. Out of these rules some have been altered to suit the needs and are contained in the Special Rules which should be read in conjunction with the General Rules. The Special Rules must take precedence over the General Rules.

1. That the name Caribbean Co-operative Enterprise be adopted as the official name of the co-operative.
2. That our registered office, for the time being, is: 177 Barford Street Highgate Birmingham B5 7EP
3. MEMBERSHIP
   Every member shall hold a minimum of ten fully paid up shares but no member shall hold or be entitled to hold more than one hundred shares in the society whether singular, jointly or otherwise, and Rule 11 of the General Rules has been modified accordingly.
   (1) Application forms will be made available as soon as possible with serial numbers so that names and monies can be registered with the co-operative.

4. SHARE CAPITAL

Shareholding held jointly shall strictly conform with Rule 3 hereof. Accordingly, each joint holder shall be deemed to hold a minimum of ten shares, and shall not be entitled to hold more than one hundred shares, singularly, jointly or otherwise.

5. BORROWING POWERS

The Directors may exercise all the powers of the Society to borrow money up to a limit of two million, in order to develop the business where the needs arise.

6. DIRECTORS

The Society shall be managed by the Board of Directors comprising fifteen Directors who shall be elected and hold office in accordance herewith.

  (i) Three Directors elected to hold office for life.

  (ii) Three Professional Directors appointed by the Board of Management from time to time.

  (iii) Four fixed term Directors appointed by the Society to hold office for the following terms:

    (a) Two for a period of five years and

    (b) Two for a period of seven years.

  (iv) The remaining Directors shall be elected by the Society in General Meeting and hold office in accordance with the rules provided hereafter.

7. The twelve elected Directors shall be elected by the members at an Ordinary General meeting held within three months of registration of the Society. In the meantime, the founder members shall act as temporary Directors and exercise all powers of Directors.

8. At the first Annual General Meeting of the Society five Directors, being neither Directors for life nor fixed term Directors, shall retire from office and in every subsequent year, four of their member shall retire.

9. The Directors to retire in every year shall be those who have been longest in office since their election but, as between persons who became Directors on the same day, to retire shall (unless they otherwise agree amongst themselves) be determined by lot. A fixed Term Director shall retire at the end of his fixed term of office.

10. Rule 58 of the General Rules shall not apply to the post of Life-Time Directors. Where a vacancy for a Life-Time Director arises, the Board of Directors shall select from amongst their number, or from amongst persons who have held the post of Director, three nominees to fill the position. Such nominees shall be recommended to the members by the Board at the Annual General Meeting or at an Ordinary Meeting at which at least 21 days notice of the purpose of the meeting is given.

11. A retiring Director shall be eligible for re-election.

12. A Director not being a Life-Time Director shall be elected by a simple majority of members present at a meeting at which due notice has been given: A Director for life shall be elected to office by obtaining two thirds of

the votes cast at a meeting at which due notice is given. Where there are only two nominees and two thirds majority is not obtained by either, there shall be a second ballot, the nominee obtaining the largest amount of the votes cast on the second ballot shall be deemed to be elected to the said position. Where there are three nominees and there is no two third majority on the first ballot, the nominee who achieved the smallest number of votes cast shall be eliminated and the second ballot shall be conducted between the nominees achieving the highest number of votes in the first ballot, and the aforesaid provisions of this rule shall apply accordingly to the second ballot.

13. The Society at the meeting at which a Director, not being a Life-Time Director, retires in manner aforesaid may fill the vacated office by electing a person thereto and, in default, the retiring Director shall, if offering himself for re-election, be deemed to have been re-elected, unless at such meeting, it is expressly resolved not to fill such vacated office or unless a resolution for the re-election of such Director shall have been put to the meeting and lost.

14. The figure three in General Rule 59 shall be substituted with the figure seven, this will represent the quorum required by the Directors before a business meeting can be held.

15. The Directors shall, from time to time, appoint a maximum of three Directors to hold office as Professional Directors. Such Directors shall be professional men or women, who shall be appointed specially with regard to their expertise. Such Directors shall be appointed and hold office in accordance with standing orders drawn up by the Board of Directors. Such a Director shall not be elected Chairman of the Board of the Society.

16. All Directors shall be subject to the Society's General Rules relating to discipline, removal and expulsion of Directors.

17. The Society shall have an Annual General Meeting in each year and , in addition thereto, the Directors may hold such other ordinary meetings as they shall from to time determine.

18. BANK
The National Westminster Bank has been selected as the bank where funds will be placed. However, if enquires are being made for the security of funds collected before the launch date and thereafter, the bank in conjunction with the Directors would act as trustees for the money until the co-operative had established its machinery to deal with its monetary business or launched business.

19. GENERAL INFORMATION
If you require more detailed information, a copy of the General Rules can be obtained on request from the registered office.

Appendix 6

YOUR TICKET TO SUCCESS

GET THE EXPERIENCE YOU NEED TO GET THE JOB YOU WANT

GET PAID, GET TRAINED, GET QUALIFICATIONS, GET JOB

HANDSWORTH BREAKTHROUGH IN CONJUNCTION WITH ADAM LTD. offers YTS training and work experience to 16 and 17 year olds' in:

- COMPUTING -
- BUSINESS ADMINISTRATION -
- CLERICAL -
- SECRETARIAL -

ADAM TRAINERS WITH PROVEN JOB SUCCESS

CALL NOW for a chat on 021 554 7982* and ask for JOHN GREY

OR write to: Handsworth Breakthrough 244 Lozells Road Handsworth Birmingham B19

AMBITIOUS?

YOUR FUTURE IS IN YOUR HANDS

WE ARE AN EQUAL OPPORTUNITIES TRAINER

(Note: The above is a copy of the advertisement used to contact clients when the project was in operation under the directorship of John Grey. Since the project was transferred from the property as stated, STEPS now offers similar services from these premises. They also plan to go into Adult Education. * The above telephone number refers to STEPS).

Entry Requirements
- You will need a reasonable standard of English to work in a commercial organization.
- Mathematical ability, to cope with basic arithmetical calculations.
- Motivation, commitment and personal presentation are seen as more important than academic qualifications.

COURSE CONTENT

20 weeks training to include three weeks induction covering an introduction to aspects of commercial work. The remaining 17 weeks training will take the form of day release.

First Year Training Will Cover General Clerical' and consists of:
- Reception and Telephone Skills.
- Office Practice.
- Basic Book-keeping and Office Statistics.
- Keyboard Skills/Typing.
- Word Processing.
- Computing—Information Technology/Use of Business Packages.
- Secretarial Studies—Speedwriting/ Shorthand.
- Law & Industrial Relations.
- Sales & Marketing

Second Year Training Will Be Specialized in the trainee's chosen area leading to recognized qualifications:

Secretarial		Clerical/Accounting
Shorthand/Speedwriting		Advanced Book-Keeping
Reception/Secretarial Studies		Accounts
Word Processing		Stock & Credit Control
Advanced Typing	OR	Data Processing
Office Organization		Principles of Payroll
Information Processing		

QUALIFICATIONS

PITMAN EXAMINATIONS (Beginners, Intermediate & Advanced)
AND
R.S.A. EXAMINATIONS (State I II & III)
Can be taken in the following areas: Typing, Book-Keeping, Office Practice, Speed-Writing, Word Processing, Data Processing and Commerce.

WORK EXPERIENCE
Every trainee will spend 84 weeks over the two years gaining practical experience with a commercial organization. These placement companies are in every area of the City and cover a wide range of offices.
Examples are as follows:
Building Societies/ Insurance Companies, Estate/Travel Agents, Solicitors, Surgeries, Industrial Offices (all above subject to availability)

BELOW IS A LIST OF SOME OF THE JOBS YOU WILL THEN BE ABLE TO APPLY FOR:

Receptionist	General Clerk
Secretary (Shorthand Typist)	Purchase Ledger Clerk
VDU Operator	Sales Ledger Clerk
Word Processor Operator	Cash Account Clerk
Wages clerk	Cashier
Tele-Sales	Copy Typist

CONDITIONS
Allowances: If you are eligible for a two year course, you will can receive £28.50 per week for the first year and £35.00 per week for the second year. A one year entrant will receive £28.50 per week for the first 13 weeks and £35.00 per week for the rest of the year. Travel costs in excess of £3.00 per week will be reimbursed by ADM

Hours: No more than 40 hours per week. You will follow the standard college, ADM or placement company hours of work.

Holidays: 18 days per annum plus all Bank/Public Holidays.

INTERVIEWS
Contact your local Careers Officer or John Grey on 021 554 7982 for an informal interview.

Appendix 7

MELBOURNE ROAD SENIOR CITIZEN & YOUTH CENTRE
(New Testament Church of God Department of Social Responsibility)

1. Name: The name of the organization hereby constituted is the Department of Social Responsibility.

2. Objects: The aims and objects for which this organization is established shall be:

a. To promote the benefit of young people, senior citizens and under fives within the City of Leicester, and with particular reference to the Highfields area, without discrimination of age, sex, race, political or religious or other opinions, by associating with local authorities and other voluntary organizations in a common effort to provide or assist in the provision of a wide range of facilities and services in the interest of social welfare and improving the condition of life amongst people.

b. To provide or establish a workshop for training of young people and the unemployed in vocational skills, financial management, book-keeping and typing, and to potential or prospective business- minded young people and the unemployed.

c. To establish or secure the establishment of a centre to maintain and manage or co-operate with the local authority and other statutory bodies, in the maintenance and management of such a centre for the activities promoted by the department of social responsibility in furtherance of the above stated objects.

In the furtherance of these objects, the department of social responsibility aims to achieve the following:

a) Reach out to people who otherwise cannot be reached.

b) Help people who would not go anywhere else, especially alienated youth.

c) Promote and support young people and their individual talents.

d) Provide luncheon club, meals-on-wheels service and craft workshops to keep them occupied.

e) Promote sports through the youth club.

f) Develop and under fives and mothers play group through stimulation, support, co-ordination and increase in the provision of facilities for children play, recreation and other leisure-time programmes.

g) Promote art and craft, and the furtherance of education in matters connected with vocational skills and to aim to develop the qualities of leadership and good citizenship.

h) This organization, in recognition of the immense value of fostering good community relations, hopes to establish close working relations with groups of similar aims and objectives; in the provision and utilization of available resources within the community.

3. Membership: In recognition of the aims and objectives of this organization, membership shall be opened to:
   i) The target groups, i.e. people who live in the inner city areas, mainly from the unemployed and one parent families.
   ii) Membership is also open to the senior citizens and the young people.
   iii) Any person who falls within this category.
4. Organizational Structure: The organization recognizes the importance of good and effective managerial principles in an organization, and places a high premium in proper planning and co-ordination of the many and varied activities undertaken by the organization. In recognition of this, the organizational structure of the department of Social Responsibility shall be divided into three sections:
   A. YOUTH CLUB
   B. SENIOR CITIZENS—LUNCHEON CLUB/ CRAFT CLUB.
   C. UNDER 5'S PLAY GROUP

A. YOUTH CLUB
This is a project which will help encourage a community spirit and to offer training, counselling and advisory services for the youth on all aspects of their lives in the following areas:
   a) Unemployment
   b) Career opportunity
   c) Social related problems
   The youth club is still in its developing stages, providing sporting activities, and the organization is constantly looking for ways and means of improvements in both the training and the facilities available.
   The youth club shall be under the supervision of a committee appointed by the department of social responsibility. The committee shall have a sole director, a secretary, a treasurer and other organizers charged with the responsibility of over-seeing the activities of the youth club, as directed by the chairman of the department of social responsibility.
   It is the responsibility of this committee that the programme and activities of the youth club are implemented, and to safeguard all the physical assets and equipments. The secretary and the treasurer shall keep proper books of accounts and records, and make sure that all moneys received are properly recorded and all expenditures are properly accounted for, and shall provide monthly reports and periodically, accounts and reconciliations.
   The youth club committee is also charged with the responsibility of bringing the needs of the club to the department of social responsibility committee.

B. SENIOR CITIZENS
Although there are several organizations which cater for senior citizens not all of them, however, belong to such groups, with particular reference to those of African Caribbean origin.

We aim to alleviate the problems of loneliness and inactivity, and also that of insecurity, and to give them a sense of belonging and usefulness. We must add that we will not confine it to just those of African Caribbean origin, but to all the elderly residents in the area.

The luncheon/craft club will be able to contribute to making their lives more eventful.

The department of social responsibility intends that the centre will be on a full-time basis (5 days per week), providing for the needs of this group.

The senior citizens club committee shall be charged with the responsibility of directing and over-seeing all the activities of the club, as planned by the social responsibility's committee, and to safeguard all the physical assets of the club. The secretary and treasurer are to keep proper books of accounts and records of membership and to account for all the monies received.

They are also charged with the responsibility to bring the needs of the club to the knowledge of the committee of social responsibility from time to time, and to promote a good image to the public about the activities of the senior citizens club.

C. UNDER 5's

There are a number of one parent families within this community, and there is a growing need for the establishment of this project.

It is the intention of this department to establish an Under 5's Play group which will deal with some of the problems that single parents encounter and which will help both parent and child. This will be two mornings per week.

We would be willing to share facilities with other groups of similar nature. The objects of this project will be to create employment, fulfilment and a place of recreation.

The play group shall have a committee appointed by the department of social responsibility committee and shall be charged with the provision of effective leadership and direction, and to suggest ways and means of improvement.

The three constituent clubs afore mentioned, namely, the youth club, senior citizens and under 5's clubs, shall constitute the department of social responsibility and shall have a chairperson. The chairperson shall have a the powers and authority to effectively direct the activities and programmes of the department.

The department shall have a committee and shall have representatives from the other clubs and other co-opted members to serve on it.

The department shall have a secretary to keep the minutes of meetings and records. All minutes shall be recorded in the minutes book, and shall be opened for inspection.

The department's committee shall meet regularly in order to review the progress and to make decisions that shall apply in any matter within the jurisdiction of the department of social responsibility.

Every proposal shall be put to the committee for vote on a show of hands, and every decision shall be by a simple majority.

In the event of an equality of votes, the chairperson shall have a second and casting vote.

The department may appoint such special or sub-committees as may be deemed necessary and may determine their terms of reference, powers, duration and composition. Such special or sub-committees shall report their actions and proceedings fully and promptly to the department's main committee.

5. Finance: The income and property of the department from wherever it is obtained shall be applied solely towards the promotion of the purposes of the organization, as set forth in this constitution, and no portion thereof shall be paid or transferred directly or indirectly in any manner by way of profit to any member of the organization. Provided that nothing herein shall prevent the payment in good faith of reasonably and proper amount as compensation or remunerations to any employee of the department (full or part time), or the repayment of out-of-pocket expenses incurred in the course of the department's business by any officer or member appointed to act on behalf of the department.

The department shall cause proper books of account to be kept with respect to all sums of money received and paid out by the department and the matters in respect of which such receipts and expenditures take place.

An account shall be opened in the name of the department at a bank to be approved by the committee into which monies received on behalf of the department shall be paid. Cheques are to be signed by two authorized officials.

6. Alteration of the Constitution: Any alterations to this constitution shall only be effective if the chairperson of the department assents to the alteration, otherwise a two-thirds majority vote at the committee meeting shall be sufficient to carry through any alterations to this constitution.

Appendix 8

OVERSTONE PROJECT—A Description
The New Testament Church of God (HQ, Overstone, near Northampton) has launched its Social Responsibility Programme of activities, one of which is the design and development of community enterprises.

To effectively assist groups (and individuals) from the Inner City areas wishing to establish business projects, but with community service orientation, the Church, an organization with Black majority members and established for 30 years, wishes to employ a research/feasibility worker who would produce a report giving information about the kinds of projects relevant to the needs of people from the Inner Cities of England and South Wales.

The Church wishes to use its resources (i.e., land, church buildings and highly motivated but unemployed affiliated persons—from within and outside its membership) to assist groups of mainly unemployed people to put their time and experience into enterprising projects, and by so doing, provide employment and reduce racial tension in Britain.

The Church is in the process of establishing links with a wide range of central and local government departments and agencies, and with a network of statutory and voluntary bodies, trusts and charities.

One example of such a link-up is that which exists between the Watts Labour Community Action Community unit of CSV and UK2000, around the project known as Overstone Project. The Overstone Project is a proposed community enterprise whereby, part of 32 acres of land at Overstone Park would be used for growing horticultural and agricultural produce. These will eventually be collected by organized units of enterprise groups which will seek to distribute the produce through contractual arrangements with public sector institutions and organizations.

Applications in writing to: Rev. E. Brown The Main House Overstone Park Northampton NN6 OAD

(The above is a sample of the advertisement for the researcher).
Overstone Project
Job Description
Post Title: Research/Feasibility Studies Worker
Department: New Testament Church of God Social Responsibility
Main Purpose of Job:
Directly responsible to and for the work of the Advisory Committee and to act upon their suggestions and advice which falls within the description of the project

Personal Duties
1. To encourage the ssetting up of units in London and other Inner City areas which will be linked to the Overstone Park Project as set out in the description of the project.
2. To call and arrange meetings of affiliated units and up- date them on progress of work.
3. To assist units to think through and write up their proposals for contracts with local authorities and other public and voluntary sector institutions and organizations; assisting the units with any queries or problems they may have in getting contractual and/or other arrangements.
4. Assisting the units to identify and gain funds from sources sympathetic to the project's success.
5. Provide information to the Advisory Committee, Social Responsibility Unit and enterprise units (if necessary through seminars) where such advice is directly related to the project as described.
6. Inform organizations, groups and/or individuals who may make enquiries about the aims and progress of the project—giving advice, if necessary, after consultation with the Advisory Committee.
7. To gather and eventually (within 6-12 months) publish a report about the feasibility of the project in the light of the level of take-up (i.e. contractual agreements) of the project
8. To implement decisions taken by the Advisory Committee (in meetings) which will monitor and encourage the progress of the researcher and the project.
9. To give information and progress reports to all organizations which contribute funds to the project (or parts of it), and such information must be done to the satisfaction of the enquiring organization and (or by other organizations who by nature of their links with the project have an interest in ensuring that such information and reports are devised and given).
Project Update
A researcher was duly found, and research on the feasibility of the project completed and duly submitted to the funding bodies. The project was then funded by City Parochial and the Barclays Bank Youth grant programme. The project is still running as a Youth Training Scheme with a full-time horticulturist and trainees. It is designed to provide training for youngsters from 17 years to 24 years. In 1991 a grant was received through the Department of Education and Science. Trainees attend a day release at Moulton College (Agricultural), Northampton. The produce are harvested and sold to Senior Citizen Day Centres and the public, and proceeds ploughed back into the project. it can safely be said that the project has provided hope for some unemployed youngsters.

Bibliography

Abrams, Philip and Brown, Richard, *UK Society* (Weidenfield and Nicolson, London, 1984).

Allport, G. W. *Handbook of Scoial Psychology* (Clark University Press, Worcester, 1935).

Alves, Ruben, *A Theology of Human Hope* (Corpus Books, Washington, 1969).

Anglican Theological Review, *American Civil Religion in 1970s* (July, 1973).

Barth, Karl. *Against the Stream,* Edited by Ronald Gregor Smith (SCM Press, London, 1954).

Bedford, Colin, *Weep for the City,* (Lion Publishing, Icknield Way, Herts., 1982).

Bent, Ans J. van der, *Breaking Down the Walls,* World Council of Churches PCR Special Report, 1986.

Berkhof, Louis, *Manual of Christian Doctrine,* (Wm. B. Eerdmans Pub. Co., Grand Rapids, Michigan, 1981).

Bieler, Andre, *The Politics of Hope,* Trans. by Dennis Pardee (Michigan. Wm. B. Eerdmans Pub. Co., Grand Rapids, 1974)

Blackman, C. W. and Secord, P. F., *Problems in Social Psychology* (McGraw Hill, New York, 1966).

Blockmuehl, Klaus, *The Challenge of Marxism,* (Inter Varsity Press, Leicester, England, 1930).

Bloesch, Donald G. *Essentials of Evangelical Theology,* Vol. 2. (Harper & Row, New York, 1978).

Boff, Leonardo, *Church, Charism and Power (SCM Press, London, 1985.*
  Jesus Christ Liberator Trans. John Drury (Orbis Books, Maryknoll, New York, 1978).

Bonhoeffer, Dietrich, *Ethics* (Macmillan, New York, 1965).

Brown, Fred, *Secular Evangelism* (SCM Press, London, 1970).

Brown, Robert McAfee, *Frontiers for the Church Today* (Oxford University Press, New York, 1973).

Brunner, Emil, *The Church in the New Social Order,* (SCM Press, London, 1952).

Campolo, Jr., Anthony, *The Power of Delusion* (Victory Books, Wheaton, Ill., 1984).

Carson, D. A., *Divine Sovereignty and Human Responsibility,* (Marshall, Morgan and Scott, London, 1981).

Chronicle & Echo, 'Breaking those old School Ties,' July, 1979.
  'Nothing To Fear,' May, 1980.

Clouse, Robert G., *The Meaning of the Millenium,* (Inter Varsity Press, Illinois, 1977).

Cobb, John B., *Liberal Christianity at the Crossroads*, (Westminster Press, Philadelphia, 1973).

Colan, Sue & Hobbs, Maurice, *New Humanity*, (BCRG, Birmingham, 1984).

Costas, Olando, *The Integrity of Missions* (Harper & Row Pub., San Francisco, 1979).

Committee for Racial Equality, Elliot House, London.

Christianity Today, Vol. 19, No. 20, July 1975.

Cruickshank, Ray, *Black People in Brent* (Hansib Pub. Ltd., London, 1987).

Dodd, C. H. *The Apostolic Preaching and Its Development*, (Harper & Row, New York, 1954).

The Parables of the Kingdom (Nisbet & Co. Ltd., London, 1935).

Dulles, Avery, *Models of the Church* (Doubleday, New York, 1974).

The Resilient Church, (Doubleday, New York, 1977).

Dussel, Enrique, *History and the Theology of Liberation*, Trans. by John Drury (Orbis Books, Maryknoll, New York, 1976).

Employment Gazette, June 1989.

Ellul, Jacques, *The Political Illusion*, Trans. Konrad Kellend (Alfred A. Knopf, New York, 1967).

Violence, Trans. by Cecilia Gaulkings (Seabury Press, New York, 1969).

Engstrom, Ted W., *The Making of a Christian Leader* (Zondervan Pub. House, Grand Rapids Michigan, 1976).

Erskine, Noel Leo. *Decolonizing Theology*. Maryknoll, New York, Orbis Books, 1981

Escobar, Samuel, and Driver, John, *Christian Mission and Social Justice*, (Herald Press, Scottdale, Pa., 1978).

Evans, Louis H., *A Covenant to Care*, (Victor Books Pub. Inc., Illinois, 1982).

File, Nigel & Power, Chris, *Black Settlers in Britain 1555-1958* (Heinemann Educational Books Ltd., London, 1981).

Forsyth, P. T. *God the Holy Father* (Independent Press, London, 1957).

Freeman, Hobart E., *An Introduction to the Old Testament Prophets* (Moody Press, Chicago, 1968).

Freire, Paulo, 'Education, Liberation, and the Church' in *A Reader in Political Theology*, ed. Alister Kee (Westminster Press, Philadelphia, 1974).

Geister, Norman, *Philosophy of Religion* (Zondervan, Grand Rapids, Michigan, 1974).

Gibson, Ashton, *A Light in the Dark Tunnel* (Centre for Caribbean Studies, London, 1985).

The Unequal Struggle (Centre for Caribbean Studies, London, 1986).

Gonzales, Justo L., *A History of Christian Thought*, (Abingdon, Nashville, Tenn., 1981).

Gottwald, Norman K., *The Hebrew Bible* (Fortress Press, Philadelphia, 1985).

Gray, Robert N., *Managing the Church* Vol. 1, Church Business Administrtion (Haymaker Press, Okla., 1976).

Green, Michael, *Evangelism in the Early Church* (Wm. B. Eerdmans Pub. Co., Grand Rapids, Michigan, 1970).

Greenslade, Philip, *Leadership* (Marshall, Morgan and Scott, Basingstoke, Hants., 1984).

Gutierrez, Gustavo, *The Power of the Poor in History* (SCM Press, London, 1983).

  A Theology of Liberation (SCM Press, London, 1972).

Harrison, Paul, *Inside the Inner City* (Hazel Watson and Vinney Ltd., Penguin Books Ltd., Middlesex, 1983).

Hill, Clifford, *Towards the Dawn* (London, Fount Paperbacks, 1980).

Holden, Tony, *People, Churches & Multi-Racial Projects* (Russell Press, Nottingham, 1984).

King, Jr., Martin Luther, *Strength to Love* (William Collins & Co Ltd., Glasgow, Great Britain, 1963).

King, Jr., Coretta Scott, *The Words of Martin Luther King* (Robson Books Ltd., London, 1984).

Kirk, J. Andrew, *Theology and the Third World Church* (Inter Varsity Press, Downers Grove, Illinois, 1983).

Klotshe, E. H. *The History of Christian Doctrine* (Baker Book House, Michigan, 1983).

Kung, Hans, *On Being A Christian,* Translated by Edward Quinn (Doubleday, Garden City, New York, 1976).

Ladd, George Eldon, *The Gospel of the Kingdom* (Wm. B. Eerdmans Pub. Co., Grand Rapids, 1975).

Macquarrie, John, *Principles of Christian Theology* (Charles Scribner's Sons, New York, 1966).

Miranda, J. P., *Marx and the Bible* (Orbis, Maryknoll, 1974).

Moltmann, Jurgen, *Theology of Hope* Translated by James W. Leitch (Harper & Row, New York, 1965).

Moyd, Olin P., *Redemption in Black Theology* (Judson Press, Valley Forge, PA., 1979).

Northampton Independent, 'Students in Residence at Overstone,' (5 May 1923).

Schubert, *Faith and Freedom, Towards a Theology of Liberation* (Abingdon Press, Nashville, 1979).

Philip, James M., *Jamaica, Its Past and Present State* (Unwin Brothers, London, 1943).

Pixley, George, *God's Kingdom* (SCM Press Ltd., London, 1981).

Richardson, Alan, Ed., *A Dictionary of Christian Theology (SCM Press, London, 1969).*

  A Theological Word Book of the Bible, (MacMillan Pub. Co. Inc., New York, 1950).

Rogers, Jack B. and Baird, Forrest, *Introduction to Philosophy* (Harper & Row, New York, 1981).

Runnymede Trust Bulletin, 'Race & Immigration,' No. (204, June, 1987).

Schaeffer, Franky, *Bad News for Modern Man* (Crossway Books, Illinois, 1984).

Smith, David, *The Fact of Racial Disadvantage* (Penguin, London, 1977).

Snyder, Howard A., *A Problem of Wine Skins: Church Structures in a Technological Age* (Inter Varsity Press, Downers Grove, Illinois, 1975).

The Independent, 17 Nov. 1987.

Third World Review, Vol. 1. No. 4/5/1985.

The Twentieth Century New Testament (trans.)

Wallis, Jim, *The New Radical Nashville*, Abingdon Press. 1983.

Weir, J. Emmette, *The Bible and Marx: A Discussion of the Hermenuetics of Liberation Theology*, Scottish Journal of Theology 35 (1982).

West, Cornel, *Prophecy Deliverance, An Afro-American Revolutionary Christianity* (Westminster Press, Philadelphia, 1982).

William, Jos. Research (Unpublished) Coventry, Clearview College of Further Education. n.d.

Wilmore, Gayraud, & Cone, James H., *Black Theology, A Documentary History, 1966-1979* (Orbis Books, Maryknoll, New York , 1979).

Wimberley, Edward P., *Pastoral Care within the Black Church* (Abingdon, Nashville, 1979).

Witvliet Theo, *A Place in the Sun* (SCM Press Ltd., London, 1985).

The Way of the Black Messiah (SCM Press Ltd., London, 1987.

Wood, Leon J., *The Bible & Future Events* (Zondervan Pub. House, Grand Rapids, 1973).

World Vision, Vol. 19. No. 6. (June 1975).

GROVE BOOKS LIMITED

publish 24-page 'Grove Booklets' once a quarter in each of the following series:

Grove Worship Series
Grove Pastoral Series
Grove Spirituality Series
Grove Booklets on Evangelism
Grove Ethical Studies

(in 1992 the prices of the first four of these Series are £1.75 each, and of Grove Ethical Studies £2.25 each)

Send for Catalogue and other information to:
Grove Books – Bramcote – Nottingham NG9 3DS
(Tel. 0602-430786   FAX 0602-220134

Of special interest to readers of *From Scepticism to Hope* will be:

ENCOUNTERING WESTINDIAN PENTECOSTALISM: ITS MINISTRY AND WORSHIP
by John Root
(Worship Series no. 66)

and

BETTER WILL COME:
A Pastoral Response to Institutionalized Racism in British Churches
by Maurice Hobbs
(Pastoral Series no. 48)